The Boy

The Brave Girls

Gary Phillips

Published by
Human Error Publishing
www.humanerrorpublishing.com
paul@humanerrorpublishing.com

Copyright © 2016
by
Human Error Publishing
&
Gary Phillips

All Rights Reserved

ISBN:# 978-0-9833344-6-0

Front Cover: Family Photo

Back Cover by:
Tom Weiner

Come with me into the woods where spring is advancing, as it does, no matter what, not being singular or particular, but one of the forever gifts, and certainly visible.

~Mary Oliver

Any form of proactive resistance is better than a lifetime of regret.

Lynn Hicks' signature

At other times I'm just a secretary: the world has so much to say, and I'm writing it down. This great tenderness

David Kirby

Table of Contents

Poetry: 1980-2016

Creative Resistance

Memory That Ole Fool

1

Up in the mountains where I'm from
There's a bald that old and round
And from its top you can see the world
Folks call it Naked Ground, yeah, folks call it Naked Ground

2

My grandpa Holloway loved to hunt coon, and he run beautiful black and tan hounds. Sometimes he would collect me from the little side-porch room I slept in, and loose the dogs, and we would roam the deep night together for hours, up-mountain and down-valley.

3

Grandma Etta was kind of a hill witch, shy and wild. It was from her that most of the Cherokee come into the Holloways, and I have a secret cunning that was transmitted directly from her to me. She's my reminder ghost that I come from a people, not just a circumstance.

4

What is memory? Memory is a stew placed over an open fire to percolate and bubble and make something of itself. Sometimes that fire is called the soul, but the stew is who we are.

5

I know about memory that it is not linear, like a road, but more like a vast boulder field of treasure and regret. I know that not even a photograph tells a tale but merely implies it.

6

For the tale includes the relationship between the teller and the seen or unseen listener, and the relationship between the listener and all the tales that construct who they are. That's my Dad there, with his sister Ethel.

7

The photograph says 1955. That's me and cousin Norma, 3 years old, buck-naked and running off to explore some wild side-stream of White Oak Creek, surely, drinking Nature and Nurture, cosseted inside a sprawling multi-racial Appalachian tribe, with wildness at every hand.

8

Memory is an old fence row running off to a mysterious location, more landmark than destination, and never ever the same place twice, now matter how vigorously remembrance imitates itself.

9

Grandma and Grandpa Phillips were sharecroppers, one of the hardest ways to make a living in this world. She come from the Price's out of South Carolina and her family was all over the color line and she was one of the great loves of my life. Lilly Price Phillips.

10

Here's Grandma and Aunt Zillie coming in from the barn after milking, taken in the 1930s. Zillie was 13 at the time. When I showed my Dad this picture he got misty and said: "That cow raised me."

11

That would be Nell, a cotton mule who entered my father's life when he was six years old and died after I left for college. He plowed a garden with her for over 30 years, beans, corn, okra, potatoes, molasses cane, turnip greens, cabbages, tomatoes, onions, pintos, peanuts . . .

12

"Along the brittle treacherous bright streets of memory comes my heart, singing like an idiot, whispering like a drunken man . . ." (e.e. cummings) That's me on the left, with my brother Carroll.

13

I don't know where this is but it reminds me of the place we killed hogs every fall. People would come from all around to help in the killing and process the meat, bringing their own knives and tools. My aunt Eulala would cook potloads of chitlins, and I would run and hide from the slaughter and the smell, sometimes for hours, once for days .

14

Memory. What happens when it flies, or scatters like a covey of quail? FDR was famous for saying "No man or force can abolish memory!" but we know him to be at least partly wrong. A thousand reasons - accident, dementia, fear - can wound memory and make it hide or adopt elaborate disguises.

15

That little girl is my mother, I know that much. Wendell Berry says ". . .our memory of ourselves, hard earned, is one of the lands seeds, as a seed is the memory of the life of its kind in its place, to pass on into life the knowledge of what has died."

16

How often do we picture the way ahead and dream of it and plan? But the actual road is never the dreamed one, and the sights we set out to see are never the scenes that we remember. It is not the cathedral that lives. It is something else, the sudden and the unexpected.

17

Not the great framed thing, but a mist, an expression on a face, a whisper.
and there is a dim glimmer of the distant lightening, and the good that one has done, and the evil. It is regret that never dies.

18

Like other Southerners I have known from the start that we would be obliged to find what it is we look for within ourselves.
ben robertson

19

This is a picture of my Uncle Junie and a friend sometime after World War II. A couple of naked men with dogs in their laps. I don't know a thing about it or what the story is. I'd love to find out.

Leaving Earth

"Freud, one of the grand masters of narrative, knew that the past is not fixed in the way that linear time suggests. We can return. We can pick up what we dropped. We can mend what others broke. We can talk with the dead."
Jeanette Winterson

Millions emigrated from Earth in the 2070s, racing the tectonic shift as the planet dissolved, as the sky disappeared in miasma, as water retreated to a third then a quarter of the earth's surface and raged there.

The destinations were chosen by lottery and outlier status. Coming from Appalachia and being of mixed race I was boarded by the anthropologists with the Revenge Societies cohort: tribal Turks, Italian hill-boys and Amazons, with a few work-booted Tennessee red-necks packing heat. Never mind that I had been a nature poet all my life and collaborated only with women. It's a miracle I survived the flight.

My great luck was that the transit-platform struck for the binary star system of Electra in the Maia Nebula, the Pleiades, which my people have always called The Seven Wandering Children.

There were those who refused to leave, and I respected them, even loved them. My granddaughter Blackberry, armored with one of the last bottles of peaty Scotch on the planet, tried to dissuade me. We clung to each other under the Terran night sky for the last time as she sang (contralto) the dark admonition of Hesiod against the Greek colonists in 750 BC:

"And if longing seizes you for sailing the stormy seas,
when the Pleiades flee mighty Orion
and plunge into the misty deep
and all the gusty winds are raging,
then do not keep your ship on the wine-dark sea
but, as I bid you, remember to work the land."

A powerful argument to me, but the land was ruined already, poisoned by the corporatocracy that won the final Market War in 2039 and declared the Earth's remaining citizens as tenants under sufferance. Buy or Die! was inscribed on our license plates, our personal identification, our house lintels,

our small and insignificant dreams.
The Earth was over, for me. I had no fight left, and too much grief, too many losses.

I wept but did not tarry, stowing into the small allotted travel bag sealed packets of watershed seeds, Octavia Butler paperbacks, a Hong Shon jade cicada, thin sheaves of poetry on handmade paper, everything indispensable, anything that reminded me of my once-insatiable love for the planet I was fleeing like a coward at the lover's deathbed.

Before leaving Earth I carefully collected my physical journals, 5 decades worth, 3 long-boxes full, and I read them carefully, then burned each one with my family and co-conspirators at a great solstice party that lasted for days.

But I saved this fragment among the few, wrapped in velum and laid in a casket with the only weapon I consented to take, a sweet gum staff from the creek below my house.

Remembering Edward:

"I remember the soft sun on the creek and Edward's pants rolled to his knees and his shouting like a boy - but then he's never met them, my own boys . . . I remember his enthusiasm at my mother's country food, his pain at the mercy-killings of the kittens, and I remember Edwards isolated fearful heart, his English way of wrapping himself like sausage around an old hurt to make a shield against new, and I remember how well he loved before he spent years on an analyst's couch, how he would say my name in a silly affectionate voice of his; which I hear in dreams, imbedded like crystal in stone. The man, though, is unapproachable, an endowed professor at a major university, an entrepreneur, an adult in therapy, a flower that bends only toward itself".

I was 31 when I wrote that, living on a homestead in North Carolina, raising soybeans and sons. So many worlds away.

News Item, Universal Press Syndicate:

Troubles continue to plague the young colony located along the Lilith Sea on the planet Electra. General Clarke of The New Militia Volunteer Armed Forces of God reported at a Tuesday press conference that the indigenous Shakori have mounted a surprising resistance to containment and removal: sabotaging urban water supplies, forming clandestine and sometimes popular rock bands to move public sympathy, attacking settlers who set fire to forestlands needed for housing and agriculture. "It's time to think about a Final Solution," reiterated General Clarke, whose daughter and wife are reported to be living in a mixed Shakori/settler art enclave in the Red Hills.

3

Memory is a net with holes, my Cherokee grandmother said. I thought it was a boulder field of regret but now, at nearly 100 year old and worlds away from my birthplace, it is light pouring into the container of my soul.

My first lover was a boy, a memory I misplaced for nearly half a century until it came riding me like a horse (early dusk by the Lilith Sea, last vestige of the shadow sun, pink waters rushing to the mangrove tide) and left me wasted, paralyzed, my feet dangling in the dangerous waters.

When I awoke there were five Shakori women standing above me, weapons stacked formally to the side. In the distance I heard shouts and gunfire. The oldest came and placed my head in her lap, oblivious to the fighting. She crooned to me until time became porous forever. I gasped. Each warrior bent willowy frame to touch my forehead, then disappeared. I could not move.

In the moment when her rough padded fingers touched me I felt such a wave of empathy that it un-manned me.

A hard-love intelligence came scouring and scrying the darkest corners of my grief, voracious, undeniable, deeply sorrowful and compassionate. I gave all, and more, delivering to our enemies the foundation for our defeat: naked desires, dreams deeper than consciousness, a compromised but ineffable love. In return she offered this fruit:

Naked tangle of sweet limbs on the riverbank, salty delicious skin, our easy laugh escaping like gas, then gasp, roiling like fishes, touching and tasting everything, momentarily stiff with contest then release, sweet release-catch-and-release, pose and repose, disclose, dispose, lean closer, close . . .

It was a memory of Marcus, who never went to school but taught me how to fish. He taught me the ritual of holding each other's hard penis and saying true things, one by one. I named my first-born after him, never exactly knowing why until Electra, the fading sun, the pink waters of Lilith.

4

Here in the floating hospital ship which is now my home, my prison, the only visitors are generals and Shakori. This took a bit of sorting out by the military bosses, but they wanted a saving-face peace, and Shakori visitors are my formal compensation.

I have been declared a non-citizen, charged by the government press as a traitor and enemy sympathizer. Having no voice, I am apparently called The Voice, and I understand there is a human cult surrounding this adventure: trainees, priests, holy whores, comediennes.

This is kept from me of course, but there are means and secret messengers, even here. Sometimes a golden tattoo will appear on my forearm after REM sleep; sometimes a tablet kindly pressed into my mouth by a warm tongue will blossom and fruit into images and words and even true tales of memory.

Gratitude flows out of me and gifts return.

5

They allow me to write one precious letter per week, my captors. Heavily censored, of course. No exhortations. Only to outworld, though they regularly appear somehow in the rebel press. Being bound, I have to write with my mouth, using a soft wooden pencil. At first each missive took me hours, but I'm getting good at it. I am not even allowed in the same room with communication technology. This makes me laugh.

I don't know if Edward is still alive or not but I have been thinking of him often. Here is my first letter in captivity:

Dear Edward,

I don't remember my grandfather's voice, but I can imagine it.
I don't remember the taste of Carole Edward's lips but I remember lying with her in a field near the old high school.

I don't remember my brother, just fragments, like slivers of glass, like a rip in the night canopy, like water running under ice. I don't remember my lies, but I remember when I began to abandon them. I don't remember my wife's tender regard for me but I know it was there and sometimes I see its ghost flicker across her face like celluloid, in dreams.

I can't remember being frightened when I was beaten by my father though I must have been. I don't remember what my first high-school girlfriend said, ever, but I remember her face in a way I could never describe. I don't remember Buell's voice but I remember her hard electric body and her flight. I don't remember our neighbor's dead son, but I know he was dark and his name was Bruce. I don't remember saying goodbye to so many people but they're gone, slipped into dark passageways or dark lives and left my ken and the hearth of my heart, gone, only the seats left in all their various architectures, only the ache remaining and my yearning like a horse at plow toward all I have loved, even you.

Even you.

6

It was the Shakori (a language like singing voices in the wind, chatter of fishes underwater) who taught me that true memory runs forward as well as backward, has a lasting physical effect on the world, their world they have chosen now to share with us and even, perhaps, with ours. This knowledge, so frightening in its implications to empire, was a gift to me for helping them find a path that did not include killing us all, boiling us out of our proud anthills, turning the world of dreams against us like a tsunami.

I gave them a key.

In a strange way, Edward, it was my unrequited love for you that was somehow the amendment stone, the wide mysterious path to my true heart which, when opened, allowed the Shakori to see our world, our desires, our slavery status, our great jagged wall of broken loves. And to be willing to live with it, with us.

7

The children came to me on a night translucent with moonlight, long hair in shiny plaits, skin-tones and faces shifting like a soft kaleidoscope through every race-memory of my family, my travels; a myriad century of true loves. It was electric. I smiled. Up came a little sexless one. She grinned and whispered: "Your body is old and will soon rest in our dust. Here is a gift. Good travels."

You and I flew over the active volcanoes of Mexico and into the largest city of the world. We are staying in the Hotel Calinda in the Zona Rosa near the Avenida de los Insurgentes, which bisects the city north to south. Just down the street is the largest mural in the world: The March of Humanity on Earth and Towards the Cosmos, painted by David Sequeiros.

Calinda Geneve is over a century old and the room is very comfortable, with a window to a hidden courtyard and a large tiled bath. Over the restaurant is a stunning glass and cast iron conservatory roof, which reflects the chaotic sounds of overlapping conversations into the lobby. I am drinking a dark brandy as I write this and they have brought me a tiny cola made with real cane sugar.

We arrived late in the day and went almost immediately to the Zocalo. Not knowing yet that Diego Rivera's History of Mexico is housed there at the Palacio Nacional, we walked the markets and then entered the great Cathedral, largest in Latin America. You my love, an atheist from Europe, were captured by the alien paradoxes of that passionate obscure Catholicism-opulence of an extraordinary nature married to great age and spiritual vision, mortared by the tears of millions of the poor over centuries.

We spent the late afternoon in that place, walking from alcove to alcove and listening to the mid-day mass under the giant vault. For the first time in Mexico, but not the last, I experienced sunlight as a physical force, as a creative and forceful entity. The day's last light played across the massive roof vaults, illuminating first a pillar of stone then a gilded saint, making a glowing geometric pattern on stone walls and domes 100 feet over our heads.

After dinner at a raucous street side café, cheap and satisfying, and then good margaritas in a bar with arched brick ceilings and beautiful tile floors, we made our pilgrims' way back to the cathedral, in order to attend a most unusual concert of the great pipe organ installed (ca.1735) in the west wing. We entered a beautiful grotesquery, with workmen pouring a slab for a new floor in the next chamber while the organ lofted Verdi to the vaults and several hundred people quietly hid and sat and milled around under the great organ and its bellows. I was impressed at the deep attitudes of reflection expressed in so many faces. I was moved. We were dwarfed and uplifted at the same time.

After the music began, attendants padlocked the giant carved oak door to the sanctuary, and no one was allowed to leave until the artist accepted our thanks from the gilded parapet above.

This morning we took a long breakfast in the beautiful conservatory room of the hotel: strong coffee, fruit, mushroom omelets and a dish of soft-boiled eggs with tortillas and red and green salsa called dramatically huevos divorciados.

How can I describe our afternoon? We entered the hotel and took our room, which was lovely and large, but dusky, the only light from a skylight above the shower and a curtained window open to the common courtyard. Tile floors, plaster walls, a niche, a large cupboard/wardrobe of some pale softwood, hard comfortable bed, wall sconces of fired clay, a wide shelf under the inset window, bedside tables, a writing table, large tiled shower.

We made love slowly and quietly for hours, several times, napping some, floating in a calm sea of our own aromas, pleasant to us, living love: touch-embrace-cuddle-hold-laugh-enter-flame and ashes, sweet ashes. "y dos cuerpos por una sola miel derrotados," whispers my Neruda: two bodies subdued by one honey. Then a climb to the rooftop garden, beer and spicy peanuts. We watched the evening descend on the city. Time, as liquid as light, spread to its thinnest canopy, languid, holy, moving and immovable. I could feel the tug of the river, even before I heard the church bells. Night like a blanket lay around us and we, like children at a party, peeked out from under and clung to each other in wonder.

Somewhere above the Pleiades an amber star beckoned to us, and we marveled at it. We slept, while Electra stitched our dreams with affection, a weft of deep longing and deeper release, an abiding and languorous peace. We slept, dreamed ourselves in different worlds, awakened, marveled, laughed.

Oh, Edward! Thank you so much for all you have given to me, past the stars and even memory.
Thank you.
Thank you.

After-note:
The poet Lord Tennyson mentions the Pleiades in his poem Locksley Hall:
"Many a night I saw the *Pleiades*, rising through the mellow shade, Glitter like a swarm of fire-flies tangled in a silver braid."

Winter Solstice 2011

Let us all stand and say: "Welcome the Light!"

Tonight we hang in balance. Like Mother Night we have been made pregnant by the Great Darkness and now we sit in vigil to birth the waxing year. If the sun agrees to return to us it will be 14 seconds earlier than yesterday, holding like a tiny seed the promise of summer.

We welcome the ancestors into our circle; we welcome into our community and spirit the whole of creation around us, the earth that sustains us and the stars above and the creatures of the field and wood.
Overhead Orion chases Taurus, the Bull of Heaven, and our Pleiades: The Seven Wandering Children of the Cherokee, Daughters of Atlas, constellation of a hundred names.

A seed moon is rising and setting with the sun and just days away from a new moon in Capricorn. Venus entered Aquarius yesterday, calling for us to dampen our emotional dramas and take a broader view of our interactions with others. The stars ask us to be adults, and kind.

Lady of the Wild Things, we honor you:
Red-winged hawks are making a harvest of first-year squirrels now that the leaf cover is down and wood chucks and eastern chipmunks have dug to their winter sleeping lairs. Noisy flocks of crows and blue-jays and robins gather at the margin of fields. The winter forms of the Hop Merchant butterfly have drunk their last drop of the year's sun and rest in diapause. Tiny screech owls are calling from the woods on still nights and soon yearling bucks will lose their antlers.

The forest floor is bright with winter's light and now subtle magick greens appear: crane-fly orchid leaves, rattlesnake plantain, wild ginger, partridge berry, running cedar, pipsissewa. We are entering the orange cast phase of the Eastern Red Cedar, when the tiny brown cones begin to color and prepare for February sex.

Not only the conifers have color; look at the evergreen angiosperms: our hollies and groundsel trees and native magnolias. There is still fruit hanging from the tree and vine in December: catbrier, sumac, roses, trumpet-vine, coral-berry, sycamores, mistletoe, and the winter buds of witch hazel, tag alder; winged elm and maple are about to swell and break dormancy and enter into the great dance of procreation.

May we too break dormancy and bloom, mine the darkness and welcome the Season of Light, Saturnalia, Dionysia.
May our words congregate and fly like the winter visitations of brown creepers and hermit thrushes and ruby-crowned kinglets, our yellow-rumped warblers, our juncos, our purple finches and white-throated sparrows.

Bonefires are burning on the hillsides of Saxony and the Goddess is afoot, talking to field and lake and wood.

Let us kindle our fire this solstice in the presence of all the holy ones...
Without malice, without jealousy, without envy,
But with the presence of the holy fire to empower us and inspire us.
May there be kindled within us this evening
A flame of love to our neighbor, to our foe, to our friend, to our families, to all.

Mountain Laurel

Wade Richmond slipped out of the Downtowner Motel in Asheville, drawn to the drumming like an Io moth riding a strand of pheromone. Wade loved drumming, even the chaotic noise he heard from the street above. Fleeing from an adventure gone bad in Mexico, he had not even carried his little djembe, but he knew he would find something to beat against in the circle, even if it was his own legs or a metal trashcan.

Wade was in his late 30s, a tall man with hazel eyes and a dancer's body. He had sold his dreads to a barber in Tijuana but kept the long brown unruly sideburns. Wade was also lost at sea, home to the mountains for a burial after 10 years of restless travel, carrying all his cash in the world locked inside a small leather satchel. He felt bruised and homeless. But somewhere near people were pounding on drums.

This was the first day of fall and Wade had only shorts and huaraches, so he took a worn blanket from the bed and made his way slowly up Patton Avenue, following the music. It was a thunder circle, hundreds of people gathered in ragged concentric rows and all drumming at the same time. Wade saw not only djembes but tablas and blonde upright congas, a couple of dunduns, bead-covered shekeres, bongos, a tall beautifully decorated ashiko flailed by a striking woman in dancer's pants and pointed slippers. He also saw rough wooden blocks and 5-gallon buckets in the fray. He smiled.

Wade surveyed the crowd and chose an empty seat beside a young dark woman trying to manipulate a hand drum while wrestling with a toddler. The two-maybe three-year old boy, brown as a berry and wearing only a cloth diaper, was playing with her long hair as she tossed it and climbing on her back and shoulders, but she persisted in her drumming, sometimes shaking him off, sometimes circling his little athletic body with her arms, nibbling his shoulders and face as he screamed in happiness.

As soon as Wade sat down the boy abandoned his mother and gave him his full attention, playing peek-a-boo from behind a large black bag on the ground and making forays to try to grab the crystal around Wade's neck. During a lull in the drumming she leaned over to take his hand in long thin graceful fingers and say: "Hi this is Jared and I'm Laurel. I have to do a gig in the circle and he's beginning to fret. Can you watch him just a minute until I get back? Don't go out of my sight, okay?" Wade looked her over frankly; she was tall, with bony slender arms and long chocolate-brown legs, high cheekbones, a sharp nose and midnight black eyes. He saw now that she was older than he first supposed. Her head was shaved closely several inches above her ears, which had multiple piercings. She smiled, unhurried.

"Sure," he said.

Laurel ran down the stairs barefoot just as an emcee with a mike was calming the crowd, not a small job.

"Who's gonna give us the word today?" the emcee intoned. "Laurel is gonna give us the word. Drum in Laurel!" Then a din arose from the crowd that was so loud it frightened the little boy and he began to cry. Wade swept him up and walked around the circle to distract him. Surprisingly the boy snuggled into Wade's shoulder and quieted, his wet face of tears penetrating the man's light t-shirt. Wade thought of his own son and held the bundle of him a little fiercely; bending his cheek to the boy's while he slept, tasting a tendril of sweet breath: spring water, beech leaf, apple scented. Wade trembled with loss.

Down below Laurel stood with her legs spread wide, a short brown lacy dress riding her thighs. Two drummers standing beside her began to make a rhythm and her voice was loud and percussive as she spoke, one syllable per beat. Wade was so astonished at her voice that he had trouble understanding the words at first, but she repeated them several times, like a chant.

Let – everything – happen – to – you (She sang)
Beauty – and – terror
Just – keep – going
No – feeling – is – final
Let – everything – happen – to – you
Beauty – and – terror
Just – keep – going
No – feeling – is - final

Wade felt like a long time had occurred, but he couldn't be certain. Laurel was standing beside him watching him carefully. Jared was asleep in his arms splayed like a rag doll. There was a din of drumming. He was in mountains. He wanted to run but the little body rooted him.

Laurel took Jared from his arms gently. "Here," she said; "Let me change his diaper and lay him down on a blanket." Wade did what she told him to, found the diapers in the large black bag and the soft cream and a plastic bag with a fresh wet washcloth in it. She unpinned Jared's diaper and pulled it away while the boy stirred but never woke. He watched Laurel at her sure graceful work, sat again on the ledge beside them.

Laurel settled the baby in and came to him. The drumming was too loud to talk. He couldn't believe Jared was asleep. Laurel handed him a beautiful tapered wooden box about 2½ feet long. The top was fine-grained walnut and the sides a blonde oak. It was tight, well-made. He admired it.

"I know you want to drum. Go ahead and use it," she shouted. "It's a Cajon made by my friend Abel Jones. And it's got a great sound!" She smiled at him again, but this time it was not a general smile. It was his.

Wade experimented with the Cajon until the drumming circle broke up. He vibrated its tapa with his fingers and drummed on its sides; he took a toy block from Laurel's bag and played counterpoint with his palm in a way he learned on the streets in Mexico. It had a rich deep sound, sometimes vibrating along his arms and migrating into his shoulders and neck. It was like massage. He closed his eyes.

Laurel was very social, talking to many people and giving soulful lip-kisses to some. He wondered if she had a husband, a boyfriend, a girlfriend maybe.

After some kind of community agreement or ritual he did not catch the drumming slowly faded and then stilled. Wade stood up and stretched, breathing deeply. Jared was awake and Laurel nursed him. Lying in the easy crook of her body he had one arm around her back and a tiny hand resting gently on the round curve of her open breast. She smiled wickedly when she caught Wade staring at her. He blushed and turned his head.

Wade was at a loss for what to do next. He walked over and gave Jared a kiss on the head, Laurel a quick asexual hug. "Well," he started; "what's next for you?"

"Listen, do you have a place we can crash tonight? It's too late to drive up the mountain and I lost my ride to West Asheville. Then maybe tomorrow you can drive us home and I'll show you something interesting. We live a little ways outside of town."

So they spent the night in his cheap room. Jared was wired from all the commotion but Laurel finally put him to sleep in the extra bed and then came to snuggle with Wade. He didn't know what to feel or do but he began to go through the motions, drawing her near to him and kissing her hard on the lips. She laughed dreamily and said: "No, it's not like that. Let's be friends. And I never make love with anybody inside of doors." She cupped his cheek and kissed him below the eyes, like ceremony. He listened to her breathe herself to sleep, his heart like a hammer, then a skittering bird against the windowpane of his anxiety. She turned him over and cupped him.

He slept some.

"A little ways outside of town" turned out to be somewhere near Blowing Rock in a place called The Globe, two hours north of Asheville. Her home was an old threadbare farmhouse held up by bushes and weeds.

They drove the white shiny rental car into the yard, haphazard with toys and plant pots and accidental sculptures. An older white man walked out the door and gave Laurel a long embrace. Wade saw that he was thin and handsome, with a trimmed white beard. He wore work clothes and a John Deere cap. Jared leapt from the car and ran to him. The man scowled at Wade, took in the rental car and spoke to Laurel: "So who's the stray?"

Wade bristled, but held himself back. He was the stranger here. "I'm just the taxi," he said.

Laurel laughed. "Wade, this is Alan. He's a farmer and he's part of our family here. And he is Jared's co-parent." She said this proudly, and Alan gave her a natural smile. "Wade is going to spend the night and I'm going to take him up and show him the glade."

Alan cocked his head and looked at Wade again. "That special, huh?"

"He's got potential."

Wade said nothing, nervous again. He had a sudden impulse to say good-bye and beg away, to not get entangled here.

They entered the house together, which was wood-floored and low-ceilinged, but the kitchen was tidy and the whole house smelled of cooking apples. "Laurel don't cook," Alan said in an exaggerated way. "I'd fix you breakfast but I'm busy with preserves."

"I'd love me some of them apples," Wade said, surprising himself.
Laurel looked at him again: "When I met you in Asheville I did not hear even a whisper of a twang. How did you get away with that?"

He dipped his head. "You know; it's an Appalachian *thang*."

Actually, his mama's homeplace was just one county away from here. He could have walked to it if he had to, on roads or not. And there was a family cemetery, which was his eventual destination. He shied from that.

Laurel slapped Alan on the shoulder and scooped from the pot a pintful of simmering apples. These she put in a rough clay bowl ("Jared and I made this.") and poured a thick goats-milk cream over it. She put a warm hand on his knee while Alan fed the toddler, and she watched him eat. He didn't know what to think, but the apples were good: spicy with some kind of pepper, buttery, tart, just hard enough to have substance. His grandmother would have approved.

Laurel was busy for a while and then came out of the back of the house with a pair of brogans and a lined canvas jacket. "Let's lite out while it's still early. I think these will fit you. Here, carry this." She held out a heavy backpack. "Alan, do you mind keeping the boy?"

He looked up from his pots: "Sure. Me and Jared will make apple butter and go swimming in the river." Jared squealed.

26

The boots were loose but the jacket was warm and comfortable. Laurel gave him an extra pair of socks and it worked. Jared stood in a chair beside Alan while he cored apples . Laurel kissed him gently goodbye and he waved her out the door. Wade followed.
She set a hard pace out of the yard and up a wide path on the hill.

He stopped. "Where are your shoes?"

She waited for him. "Come on. I'll tell you all about it while we hike."

"Have you ever read Born to Run?" she began. "Great book. It changed my life. Shoes are a terrible invention and actually hurt your feet. They cause us to walk in unnatural ways and to lose contact with the ground. It's very important to feel the earth."

He quickened to keep up with her. They walked briefly side-by-side until the path narrowed and entered the woods. "Did you know Geronimo ran barefoot 50 miles across the Mojave to steal horses? Do you know about the Tarahumara, greatest runners in the world? They run up to 100 miles at a stint and never wear more than thin sandals. Being barefoot means you are gentler on your legs and step correctly, among other things."

He listened to her chatter and wondered, watching her brown legs and bare feet as they danced down the rocky mountain trail. He had avoided shoes whenever possible until he was a teenager, so he understood a part of what she was saying.

After a while Laurel took a more relaxed pace and was mostly silent, except to point out flowers and plants and interesting trees. Wade had been well-schooled by the mountain women in his family; he knew his people's names for many native plants. He also knew old stories and the uses of things, though it had been many years since he had studied attentively with his grandmother.

Wade was usually shy about this, but with Laurel he felt no reluctance, stopping by cohosh and Indian pipe (corpse plant, his granny called it, deepest medicine of the Cherokee) and musky galax, collecting pig-nut hickories from the forest floor, climbing a dead poplar to cut away a clump of oyster mushrooms. These he started to put in a plastic gathering bag but she said no, it's disrespectful to put mushrooms in anything other than a basket and she produced from the pack on his back a clever little collapsing container woven with string, which she carried up and down the mountain.

Wade's anxieties were still present and clung to him doggedly but they abated in the woods and he began to relax a bit. He surprised himself by missing his birth family for the first time since he retreated back to Appalachia, thinking of his luminous grandparents and his aunts and uncles and all his cousins, the almost-always loving, mostly good people who had made him and who he had abandoned without a word for years. A wild rush of feeling unnerved him suddenly. He sat down in the leaf litter and put his head in his hands, which were shaking.

When he looked up Laurel was on her haunches very close to him, eyes averted respectfully but attentively. He sighed audibly, but she touched his lips and shook her head. "Feel what you feel," she said gently, hauling him to his feet.

"Wait'll you see this!"

They climbed over a ridge and down into a deep bowl filled with enormous trees: poplars, white oaks, a stand of thick beeches circled like sentinels; majestic hemlocks lined the upper slopes. He saw hundreds of pawpaws in a gold explosion along the deep creekbank, laurel hells marching up the farther hill, colonies of dog-hobble, a solid slope of black cohosh, trillium, bearberry and more.

Wade breathed deeply. It was beautiful. Beside him Laurel's eyes suddenly filled with tears. He pulled her to him reflexively, nestled her head into his chest, whispering assurances while his heart started and battered. Her voice came to him, muffled inside the fold of his jacket:

"We fought like dogs to save this place, testified at every Forest Service hearing, had demonstrations, climbed these trees when the loggers came. We laid down in front of the bulldozers . . . We thought we were warriors." She looked up. "We won. We beat the Forest Service and the loggers. We were on television." Her voice rose: "And then the fuckers clearcut half the Globe, all the way from here to Blowing Rock. It's a horrible mess.

God damn the sons-of-bitches."

After that he had to hear the whole story, and she had to rest with her head in his lap to tell it, then she walked him to the vast clearcut nearby, raw red earth, deep-cut roads, bulldozer burn piles, worse. He could feel her rage like a flame, not knowing whether to stand near it or away from it. "You have to see this to see all of it if you want to see me. This is my home."

The sun began to dip behind the highest ridge and the mountains were carved into dark and gold. "Hurry," said Laurel. They hiked quickly through the corner of the clearcut and forded a rocky creek, then climbed over the next ridge. Down below and glowing under sun's last light was an old apple field. He saw there was a camp, with lean-to, wide tarp and a firepit with cooking utensils.

Laurel opened a blanket chest in the lean-to. "I'll make the bed," she said. "You walk down that little road to the spring and see what's there for us to drink. Here, fill this with water." She handed him a glass jar.

The spring was further away than he imagined, and it was almost dark before he found it, a perfectly round stone-lined bowl nestled into the base of a giant buckeye. There were leaves on the top of the water and these he brushed aside before he filled the jar. The water was ice-cold and he drank half of the first fill before he topped it off. Under the water were several glass containers and he took them up one by one and tasted them. The first was a cheap jugwine and this he put back in the spring, but the next container tasted much more interesting; fruit and herb and honey, not sweet really, but with a strong fermentation nose. He hauled it out. He took out too a little jar of homemade peach brandy. Not bad. He thought of his grandfather, who would have smiled and said "sharp as a knife and clear as moonlight." He tasted the shine again before he gathered the bottles together. Wade hesitated beside the buckeye tree, thanking it and the spring as he had been taught. He took up a shiny hard buckeye nut and put it in his pocket.

It was awkward carrying the 3 bottles in the dark, but he found the path by following a slim opening in the sky above. Up at the camp a little fire was burning and Laurel was sitting by it, a blanket across her knees.

He sat, nearby but not close, looking into the chattering fire.

Laurel waited patiently for a while then slid over next to him and took the peach brandy from his lap. She took a long slow pull from the jar: "There's a story about this shine. For one thing it's made in the basement of the Mountain Laurel Primitive Baptist Church. No shit."

Wade laughed. It felt good to laugh. Laurel said: "You can drink as much as you want of this, but be careful. It might impair your judgement." Next she brought out from the lean-to tall glasses. "Here, let's hit some of Alan's rosemary mead."

They sat and drank from both bottles for a long time, watching the moon's progress and listening to coyotes place-calling and howling. They seemed very close. He had never grown up with coyotes, but he liked the sound; it felt like a bridge between northern Mexico and his mountains.

At some point Laurel picked up a lantern and walked down to the creek to take a bath. He waited a minute and then followed her, watching from a corner of one of the big apple trees at the bottom of the meadow. He suspected Laurel knew, because she made a show of taking off her clothes slowly and walking into the cold water with a bar of soap. His breath caught, watching her naked body silvering under the lamplight. Laurel washed herself slowly in spite of the cold, humming a little, laughing some, leaning up toward the emerging moon with open arms before she turned toward him and said: "Go ahead, take your clothes off and wait for me under the covers. I'll finish getting myself ready for bed." She smiled.

Wade stood up abruptly and walked to the campfire, stripping quickly (damn! It was cold) and crawling under a stack of quilts near the fire. He waited, not sure what he wanted.

Laurel slipped off her cotton dress and lay beside him like a dark silvery fish. She giggled softly and bedded into him, weaving one slim brown arm under his neck and resting her forearm on his chest. She began tracing slowly and carefully his face, his deep forehead and wide ears and sharp arching nose, stroking his rough beard with her delicate fingers. She brought up a leg and placed it across his upper thighs, close enough to his sex that his scrotum could feel the warmth of her skin. He tingled deliciously but did not harden.

Wade could not believe how close she was, and how graceful and sure. It was the closest physically he had been to a human being in four long months, three of them spent in a small Mexican prison. Wade looked at the full moon and began to weep. He tried to do this quietly but could not hold back the sobs that swept over his body like a tide.

Instead of withdrawing Laurel held him firmly but even more gently, riding his waves of grief like a skillful and compassionate horsewoman.

When he relaxed and looked about him the moon had progressed by 10 or 15 degrees. Laurel touched his lips for silence and lay beside him for a long while. Every time he bent to move or speak she stopped him, saying: "No, this is not the time yet."

He realized at some point she was tending him, slowly and methodically cupping and holding parts of him, touching gently others, somehow managing and communicating with the moving disparate energies of his body. He had a momentary panic at this and felt himself tense, but Laurel smiled and kissed him gently on the cheek. "For tonight," she said, "do not worry. Do not anger. Be filled with gratitude." He gave himself over to her. He felt the gratitude.

At some point she unlaced herself from him and sat beside him on her knees, holding her hands a few inches above his body, moving them slowly from his head to his feet, chanting softly the names of glands and body parts.

"What are you doing?" he asked.

"Shhh. I'm scanning you. Man, you have got some shit going on in your root chakra!"

"Root what?"
"Hush. Let me finish."

31

Laurel eventually nestled back into his side. She stroked the long hairs of his chest and stomach then cupped her warm hand over his penis. No response. He started to apologize. "Hush!" she whispered. "He's had a workout you don't even understand. Leave him be." She curled around him and fell asleep, snoring softly on his shoulder. But she still held his penis, softly but firmly.

The moon was high overhead when he awoke, dreaming of making love with his wife Nathalia in the desert wash above Mineral de Pozos. In his dream animals gathered around them quietly and without malice. He saw night lizards, scorpions, coyote, jackrabbit, rattlesnake, pygmy owls. In his dream he was counting the animals one by one while he entered her from behind on the desert floor. He had no fear.

Wade opened his eyes. His penis was rock-hard from REM sleep and still captured in Laurel's hand. She was wide awake and grinned at him. "Gotcha." she whispered. He watched as she gave him a long licking caress and then mounted him, massaging her labia with spit and guiding him into her soft wet vulva, tightening around him in a kind of kegel exercise that startled him. She sat up with all her weight on his pelvis and stretched luxuriantly, cat-like. Behind her body he could see Orion and Taurus and the Pleiades.

She positioned herself to have an orgasm on his pelvic bone which she did with great fanfare and exultation then collapsed against his chest with a grunt. He wrapped his arms around her back, reveled in the feel of having access to so much of her body above him, slowly began a new rhythm that carried hers ("Fuck me til I sweat," she said), had a second explosive orgasm after they made each other wet as seals. She rolled off him. He slept his first real sleep in days.

And woke to a blinding sun. Laurel sat beside him cross-legged. She was dressed in nothing but a thin t-shirt and one of the quilts. "I've been watching you," she said.

"I'm wondering what a child of yours would look like."

"Last night I was in the middle of my estrus cycle, sweet Wade; my fertile window was wide open."

"What?" Wade was still groggy, trying to capture the elusive tendrils of last night's desert dream and sex with Laurel. His mind was mixing them up.

She smiled. "It is my earnest hope and wish that we made a baby last night." She nestled against him and touched his cheek.
Wade shook his head and abruptly sat up. Shit! One day in the mountains and he was saddled with a barefoot possibly-pregnant probably-goofy hippie girlfriend. He suddenly felt sick.

Laurel eyed him carefully and then withdrew and threw his pants at him. "You sink back into your misery so fucking fast," she said. "Get up; let's walk."

After he dressed she took his hand and walked him down to the path to her garden. They were much closer to her house than he imagined. He had offered to pack up the camp but she said no she'd come back later and spend the day with Jared here; he liked to swim in the creek and she could be alone with her feelings.

He felt embarrassed. Laurel put her arms around him and pressed her forehead to his. She was nearly six feet tall in her boots. "Listen," she said; I ain't looking to tie you up. This decision was mine alone and I'll not let you take the joy out of it."

"Jared is mine and nobody else's; his daddy don't even know he exists, and that's the way I want it."

When he tried to speak she put a finger to his lips. She spoke again, more slowly. "I did you a courtesy here by telling you my intentions because I'm developing a genuine affection for you in spite of your liabilities, but I'm not looking for a man around, or a helping hand, or anything other than what you've already given me."

"Now get your sorry sad ass on back down the mountain and do whatever work it is that you came here to do. "

"I forbid you to see me for six months, Wade. I like men but I don't like them messing with me and I ain't going to be your continuing compensation in this new world nor your distraction from some of the shit you have brought down on yourself. Be brave. Goodbye."

They had arrived at the cabin and Jared came running to his mother. She kissed both his cheeks and they turned away, never looking back. He looked at her roommate Alan, who had listened in on their exchange. "Is she always like that?"

"Yeah she is." Alan grinned. "Glorious, ain't it?"

Wade walked slowly to the rental car. The hood was covered in tiny paw-prints, but the kitten did not emerge from under his seat until he was south of Linville, sun just above the Black Mountains, maple-tips ablaze along the roadside, just a few miles away from the house his mother had been born in.

He placed the tiny warm body between his legs, where it settled quietly. Wade Richmond turned off onto the small road that wound up the Cane River and eventually led to Big Creek. There would be people there who would be glad to see him, regardless of his condition. They needed him, and he needed to be needed. He wanted a connected life again. He would earn it.

Laurel would approve. He wondered what she would think of his chaotic family. He would find out, in six months.

Spring Equinox

Vernal, I say:
First Point in Pisces.
Inanna's Return.
The festival of Nowruz.
Talking about love, here on the edge of the northern equinox
Green sprouts breaking ground like orgasmic exclamations
mate-call drumming- pileated, downy, hairy, red-bellied
Chorus frogs and cricket frogs exulting at all hours
woods colored in trout lilies, saxifrage, bloodroot, wild cherry
At night I can sense earthworms processing fertility,
the daughters of Atlas rising to hold their place
enticing whispers of nesters and burrowers
Tonight I'll leave my empty bed
Follow the creek to the first toadsong
Watch as wild garlic seduces the moon
Break open my heart and
Get my feet wet

My Grandmother

Knew the sacred nature of her place
A scrap of mountain above Cane River, on Big Creek,
the blue ridge a bowl above the barns
I remember holding a handful of her skirt to keep up,
hunting creasy on a February morning
our breath like the smoke of campfires
 air uncurling in the tiny valley, snaking
its slow way up the hills
almost visible
Much of my grandmother's life was like that, almost visible
We walked together
I was proud to be with her, knowing her importance
She pointed out the sacred places
Among the rocks and pathways, under stone and by water
The trees of worth
The shy creatures of air and earth and sky
She let me see they
Meant no harm
Had their own ways
And business to perform
We sat at the top of things
Before the biscuit bag was opened
Together, looking down at her valley
My hand in her lap
Mist rising in prayer-tatters
Above the silver shining river

To The Spirit On My Shoulder

It probably began in the Holloway family cemetery. A tangled square surrounded by an iron fence and inhabited with stones and a single tall jack pine, high above Big Creek and his family's homeplace.

Robbie had flown in from a trip to Mexico for the funeral of Aunt Lilly, one of the twins. He had carried her sister Millie up the steep pasture ahead of the family, where they sat beside each other on the tombstones and talked, arm in arm.

It was a simple ceremony, at the end of which a distant cousin began keening Will the Circle Be Unbroken. Her voice was untrained and her accent thick as burley rosin, but emotion palpated his heart. He wanted to sing with her but he was shy-it felt indecorous. On the second verse (But I could not/hide my sorrow/when they laid her/in the grave) another voice chimed in from the east corner under the pine, a woman's, reedy but clear, and so he began to sing too, pouring out his heart over the hills.

Afterward, the family gathered on the long front porch of his Uncle Virgil's house. He was appreciated for singing but no one confessed to hearing that second voice but him. Not a soul. Aunt Millie gave him a long hug and whispered: "It was Lilly you heard, darling. She always did like to sing."

So it was that after he drove home to the flatlands his grandmother Etta began appearing to him. It was from her line that the Cherokee came into the Holloways, and he had spent long summers with her in the mountains, following her around like a shadow as she cooked on a wood-fired stove, collected herbs and greens, made poultices and cures, and met with little covens of other dusky women. It was in these meetings that his grandmother lost her silent shy aspect and spoke intimately and with a certain respected power. He loved his grandmother above all others; she was his best friend.

And she had come to him in a dream the night she died. He was 12 years old and at summer camp. In the dream she carried him through her little mountain house, slowly and lovingly through every room, but when they came to the bedroom her bed was empty, the covers undisturbed. By this he knew she was gone.

He had often thought of her, wrote poetry in her honor, acknowledged to friends and others her influence on his life and character.

The process of her actual habitation was gentle: from rich memories to silky whisperings to a physical presence. Now he felt like her spirit perched on his shoulder at times, during ceremony in particular but also when he enjoyed experiences unfamiliar to her.

His grandmother spirit had a wry sense of humor and was full of opinions. She was fascinated by his women friends. Sometimes when he met a woman for the first time his grandmother would "read" her or insist that he deliver intimate messages to her, which caused him some trouble.

3 Stories:

1

In central Mexico he met a young painter who was a friend of friends. They had a warm intelligent conversation on the balcony above an arroyo, a green strip of dry riverbed. As they talked he saw 2 coyotes emerge and lope up along the channel away from them. Into his ear his grandmother insisted: "Tell this woman that her deformity is also her strength; that she must not have an operation to correct her foot. If she does it will plague her and sap vitality from her. She must learn to love the parts of herself that shame her, for they carry her sense of character."

This was a message he could find no way to deliver, so he ignored his grandmother. He imagined he could feel her petulance and withdrawal. Robbie and the Mexican artist agreed to share Facebook. A year later he saw a picture of her wan face bravely smiling from a hospital bed: "My recovery from surgery is taking much longer than I thought. All of this has been an intense ordeal." Robbie suffered an irrational stab of guilt.

Alexandra invited Robbie to visit her family in Portugal, so he did. There she proudly introduced him to her best friend from elementary school, a slim woman named Elena. They all shared a bottle of wine on the back porch steps, the moon a silver crescent above the farm fields.

His grandmother buzzed: "Talk to her about her sadness. Tell her that her search for sanctuary is not lost or wayward. She deserves a safe place to call her own and create an atmosphere of beauty that nourishes her; she has that right. She has that responsibility, for she will make sanctuary for others."

He decided this dispatch was safe enough to broach, since he nor the other woman spoke each other's language. When his friend walked inside for another bottle of wine he began to transmit his grandmother's message in English, gamely but somewhat embarrassed, holding his wine glass and speaking in a friendly tone. The woman looked at him intently and took his free hand in both of hers. He faltered but continued. She burst into tears.

Suddenly Alex was standing above him. "What the hell is this?" she said, and helped her friend into the kitchen, looking back at him reproachfully from under the porch lamp.

He never saw Elena again, but his Portuguese friend, still baffled, carried warm regards from her each time she visited her family. And almost exactly a year after his visit a thin volume of revolutionary songs by Ana Luisa Amaral was forwarded to him from Lisbon, without note or signature.

3

He became bolder about acknowledging this spirit presence, mentioning his grandmother in his poetry and speaking her name sometimes in introductions. To his astonishment some people accepted this perfectly.

At a writers conference in Vermont she pestered him about a

woman in his workshop, a brooding Italian professor who had written a compelling lesbian love story set in the bioluminescent bays of Puerto Rico. It was his favorite piece, and he admired the writer.

This woman gave him a good and serious critique of his science fiction short story, handing him afterwards the notes she had written in his margins. When she read her own story the next day he was reluctant to comment, battling with his own feelings and his grandmother's perceptions, which he could find no basis in.

The writer forced the point, looking at him and asking: "What did you think of it? I really want to know." He hesitated. Perhaps in this safe space he could be absolutely honest.

"I have to go elliptically at this," he began. "And I have to ask your permission to do something strange. You know already that I participate in and lead ceremonies, that I am a religious and have a spiritual discipline. I also carry a grandmother spirit on my shoulder, my own grandmother in fact, a Cherokee woman from the mountains of North Carolina. And she has a message for you. Do you want to hear it?"

She nodded, smiling slowly. The workshop leader, a much-admired poet from northern Mexico, whistled: "Well, this is a first. My Yaqui ancestors are crowding into the portals of my eyes!"

Robbie began slowly:

"She says this is a great story, an important story, but you have been about the business of de-constructing it far too long. She says you need to stop building walls against the work you must do, or you will wither within those walls. She says to stop editing and re-editing. Go ahead and release it; there is an animal spirit behind it that is more important than this little story; it is your life."
"Does that make sense?" he asked, suddenly feeling vulnerable and spent.

The table was silent. The writer nodded slowly. "I have at least five other versions of this story. And I just decided to consign this one to the trashcan. I feel I can't write anything else until I completely finish it. Yes I understand. Thank your abuela for me."

The class was very quiet.

Robbie felt a warmth on his shoulder,
like a ray of sun against his living skin.

Summer Solstice at Megan's 2014

Let us all stand and say: "Welcome the Dark!"

Tonight we hang in balance. Like Persephone we have been made fecund by the summer light and now we sit in vigil to birth the waning year. If the sun agrees to return to us it will be 14 seconds later than yesterday, holding like a tiny seed the promise of winter.

We sing a love letter to the southern Piedmont, a hymn of particularity, a nature song for every wind and leaf and rich wild birdsong, for the killdeer nesting in Megan's field, for the barn swallow foraging the air above us, for the little green heron in the shallows of the pond, for all:

The sun entered Cancer this morning and will occupy the Silver Gate between Taurus and Gemini for three days. Not only is Mercury in retrograde but by month's end so will be Saturn, Pluto, Neptune and Chiron. Our carefully constructed structures of separation are being exposed and broken apart. Do not be afraid of the shadow because that is where courage abides.

Tonight Castor and Pollux the Twins will rule the horizon and Orion the southern sky. Antares shines in Scorpio and noctilucent clouds ride midnight. Earthshine may be visible tomorrow. Polar day rules above the arctic circle, where the sun will not set for 24 hours.

In our bioregion deer are browsing the tops of mandrake root - box turtles have laid their eggs and will congregate to rest the summer together in moist seeps and dry bed - black - winged damselflies travel streambeds and snapping turtles are on the move.

Blooming: butterfly weed, poke, mimosa, Carolina hemlock, passionflower, wild roses, elderberry, button bush and trumpet creeper. Mullen is near to flower, and yellow jewelweed. Carolina wrens and tyrant flycatchers are tending second broods.

Blackberry season is just beginning and persimmons are blessed with a flush of first green fruit.
Season of the Sun and season of the soul: Let Gaia be at the heart of all we do at this time, every drumbeat, every heartbeat, every circle. May women's

wisdom guide us and let all who are greedy stand aside.

The world is alive. We who are here gratefully gather in a sacred manner to celebrate the turning of the year and to sing our heart-song to the southern woodlands that surround and shelter us: hickory and white oak, sourwood and pond pine, beech and sweet gum, ironwood, live oak, river birch, silver maple, cypress, black walnut, tulip poplar, black willow, brave chestnuts, dogwoods, and all their allies.

May we become indigenous to our places and make treaty with the trees, shelter them as they have sheltered us, protect the places of the old ones, treasure every copse and thicket, every weald and wood, pocosin, grove, woodlot and orchard.

May we all enter together into the arms of sleep tonight blessed and protected and filled with wonder, listening to the whispers of the trees.

Now let the people say Aho!

The Morning Of Our Abortion

The morning of our abortion was windy and warm. From the bay window of a little trailer on the marsh I watched the sea grasses moving and shrimp jumping in the narrow creek. A marsh hen ventured out on stilt-legs to capture a crab on the mud bank, then disappeared. Our neighbor Tom was mending nets, singing to himself under the fish shed. I finished my coffee and left the window reluctantly.

On tiptoes at that window I could just see Drunk Jack Island and the open ocean, less than half a mile away. Between us and the big water ran the salt creek, 20-30 feet wide by our place and opening to nearly a hundred out in the open channel, depending upon the tide.

Across the parking spot squatted the oyster roast owned by our landlord Morse, with its boat ramp and fish shed. The oyster roast was old style, long tables with holes in the middle and trash cans to catch the shells. He kept a simple menu: oysters, shrimp, corn-dodgers and beer. There was a Coke machine across the parking lot to serve non-drinkers.

Morse rented out boats for cash in the off-season, mostly small wooden fishing vessels. I kept one of his oyster boats to use, solid cypress, hand made and heavy as a small car. Morse had two Gullah men who worked digging oysters out of the creek bank. Their laughter was musical and sometimes we would share a pint of whiskey in the evening if I wasn't working, quiet out of respect for that magic time when the marsh puts on its fire colors and all the sounds seem to deepen to bass notes. Janet would come home from work and join us. Time was seamless. We were a boat rocking at its moorings on a calm day, those dusky evenings.

Were we 21 yet? I can't remember. It was the first time I had ever lived with a woman. It was the first time I ever made a household, loved it, cared for it. We told Morse we were married, but his wife looked at me with open distrust and gave her sympathy to Janet. She and I were experimenting with love, living on tips, captured and conquered together by the estuary, the marsh, the deep rich Carolina wetlands outside our door. Far away from all the other lives we knew.

Janet crept from the little bedroom off the hall. Her blue kimono hung loose over freckled skin, open at the neck where sun lines made a sharp distinction under the falling red hair, which she swept back now out of habit. She had large green eyes and a man's rough hands. She was shy in a way, quick to retreat, slow to bear grudges, but strong, firm, guided by an inner vision of her life which did not depend upon me for its validity.

The night before had been tender and fragile-no lovemaking; we were a pair of scared kids holding each other in the dark. She opened a window to the sounds of the marsh and we talked for hours, quietly, like conspirators, criminals of love.

I made a breakfast of cinnamon toast and eggs, taking coffee to her by the table. Janet had a plan. We were going to a clinic in Columbia, at least two hours away. She had made the appointment. She knew what she had to do. At the table she was quiet and withdrawn, watching the creek and the marsh birds and Tom at his nets.

When the time came we hurried to the car. The wind had risen some and seemed to chase us from the yard. We drove without event to the city, sat in a waiting room together for a while, then she was taken to a place I could not go. I felt lost in the waiting room, fiddling with old magazines and stifling my impulse to walk away. Janet came out eventually and we left. I drove her little Rambler and she leaned against the window, holding herself and napping while we rode the flat coastal plain of Carolina. I worried.

We stopped for lunch at a Chinese restaurant but Janet couldn't eat, so we bundled our food in boxes and left quickly. By the time we hit Lake City the wind was up and I could feel it rock the little car, but we didn't find out about the tropical storm until I stopped by the restaurant. Janet had arranged to have the day off but I was scheduled to wait tables for the night shift. I wanted to see if I could come in late or get somebody to work for me. Only Barbara was there, closing the cash register and locking doors.

"What's happening?" We had been too preoccupied to notice the atmosphere of haste and anxiety in the village.
"Don't you know? The biggest storm of the season is about to hit and everybody's closing down. You might as well count on losing electricity tonight. Be careful getting home."

I helped her close the building and we hurried to the trailer, stopping only at Jack's store for beer and bread. I had to pound on the door to get his attention. The old man said: "Gonna be a bad one," and started hammering the storm shutters.

Rain started driving in hard sheets and our visibility was terrible. We were desperate to be home. At the Chandler house I noticed a live oak down across the drive. The roads were empty.

By the time we got to the trailer the salt marsh had disappeared and the hungry ocean lapped at our yard, twenty feet from the picture window. We sat in the little metal house while the wind rocked it so hard that glasses fell and our large aquarium imitated the motion of the sea.

I secretly believed our anguish had created the storm.

A sudden pounding on the door: It was Morse, drenched to the skin and looking like a watery ghost. "My boats!" he cried, shouting over the storm: "My boats!" We looked out the door to see Morse's precious boats breaking their moorings in the wind and floating out to sea. I saw Janet spring from the table. She somehow rushed past me and toward the water, soaked by the rain in the first few steps. I followed, and for an hour we waded and swam after the old man's heavy oyster boats.

When the last boat was recovered we followed Morse into his low concrete house and waited out the storm, drinking whiskey from a bottle at a table by the window. Janet sat, relaxed and shy, her leg across my thighs under the table, her hand naturally draped across the back of my chair. Outside, the storm withdrew slowly, with a thousand whispers. We walked across the gravel lot in a world fresh-scrubbed, tender but alive. Making for home.

Fall Equinox

Watching fall come
to Silk Hope is like spying a dear friend from a distance.
Every nuance and shading,
every tiny event,
has a resonance to it, an anticipation of joy.

light and darkness balance
what are our blessings?
what hard questions will we carry into the solitude of winter?

Scorpio and Sagittarius along the elliptic
Vega, Deneb and Altair
Argiopes tie up their final eggsacs and desiccate
Luna moths are dying
hummingbirds leave on a long journey
last songs of snowy tree crickets, cicadas, katydids,
praying mantises build hard egg cases
in the memories of their grandmothers
harvestmen, mating in a fever, gathering in masses
grey squirrels-cold-day leaf dreys just big enough for two.
monarchs on the wing to Mexico gather on grandmother trees
a thousand generations old
chimney swifts swarm on Crowder's Mountain
hawks begin migration
corvids gather in fields
mourning doves call in the twilight
great horned owls practice-sing
                        every animal is crepuscular.

Foraging: maypop, persimmon, muscadine, moccer-nut, the first
succulent shelves of fall oyster mushrooms
Beech-nuts are worth competing for

Tupelo is turning: black gum, swamp tree, longest living non-clonal
flowering plant in Eastern America
Sycamore, poplar, red sumac
flowering boneset, rabbit tobacco, false foxglove, partridge pea,
hearts-a-bustin', witch hazel.

May nature share her bounty; may we enter into the arms of this night alive as the world is alive; vibrating, generous and kind.

The Way Love Circles

I believe I can remember the first time my father was really angry with me.

We were going to the store together. I sat in the front seat with him, on a long upholstered bench big enough for four. My habit was to slide over close enough to touch him. I might put my hand on his big leg for comfort, or lean against his body if I was sleepy. Sometimes I sat straight and tall to peek over the dashboard. We talked. I was five years old.

The car was a two-tone green and white 1956 Chevy. Before this there was a blue '49 Mercury, the first car my father ever owned and his transition from mule and wagon days to a man who boarded in town and carried in his pocket stiff cotton-mill cash. Then he met my mother, an irrepressible generous mountain girl with a pin-up poster body, and she got pregnant, probably in the Mercury coupe. They got married. I was born several months later.

So my father traded in the Mercury for a four-door family car, but he described the coupe so well and so lovingly to me that I can almost think I knew it. I can imagine myself captured in my mother's arms for safety or sleeping in the wide back seat of that luxury world which was my father's first taste of owning something fine, him still close in the shadow of the boy who went barefooted to school, who got oranges for Christmas if he was lucky, whose father took him out of the eighth grade to make him walk behind a mule for fourteen hours a day.

We are driving to the store, my father and I, and I am sitting close beside him on the long bench seat. My hand is resting on his lap and I am excited: we are going to the store. The store is the only store I know, a rambling old frame building at the crossroads of Green Creek, with a high porch, dark wooden floors and a fat round wood stove. The wood stove is always surrounded by white men in overalls, kind men mostly, at least to me, men who daily pass judgement upon the workings of the world as they take turns opening the stove door to spit tobacco juice into the fire. I can hear the sizzle; I can smell the wood smoke and tobacco runnel.

I want a treat. I need a nickel. When Daddy says: "No, you can't. Now get along while I pay for the gas," I am not disappointed. I have friends here. I walk into the circle of old farmers and beg a coin. They give without a pause, a good-humored laughter their reward for the generosity of the moment. They know my father; they respect him. They know me from the store banter of everyday. They all want to act my grandfather; it's the way of the country world, where family extends into familiarity and all life's connected to locality with a thick rope of communal love, at the best of times, or hard-edged and deadly prejudice at the worst.

I walk up to my father with an ice cream bar in my hand, triumphant. When I reach for his hand I see dark clouds gather in his face and I am confused, lost. I wait, still as a cat.

"Where did you get that?" He has my other arm in his hand, the one that does not have the ice cream.

I point to the men around the stove, who are silent and watching. I see them rise in their bodies as if to attention and say (I know that only one man speaks but somehow it seems as if all are speaking): "Aw, it's okay, Gurley . . .He just . . .," and something else but I cannot listen because my father has turned his attention to me again, and I am afraid of him.

He makes me take the ice cream back to the grocer and exchange it for the nickel and take the nickel to the men while he leaves the store without me. When I climb down the long steps of the porch with tears in my eyes he is waiting, still storm-faced.

On the ride home I hug the door at the other side of that bench seat while he says over and over: "Don't ever do that again. Don't you ever beg money from strangers again, or I'll stripe your legs so hard you won't sit for a week. Do you hear me?" I hear him, staring out the window to the farm fields and the barns and the cows.

I puzzled this knot for years, puzzle it still. How can a person who loves you and nurtures you give you harm? Love and hurt can be so closely twined, like a snake around a stick. It happens too at the other end of that dark tunnel: the child who hates you just for a minute, the scorn in his eyes when he looks at you across a table, a room, a world.

Sometimes love is hugging ourselves until we come to, come around, consciously uncurling our body from its stick of fear. Sometimes love is leaping across the spaces of our fear to find the other shore, the far green country, if only for a while. In love, we wait. In waiting we love.

My father helped me with this, sitting a full generation later in the same kitchen we returned to when I was five years old. He told the story to me while my own boy slept in my lap, the story of a young scared father who felt humiliated and angry at himself because he didn't have a penny in his pocket past the gas money to get himself to work, who couldn't give his son a nickel because he didn't have a nickel, not in his pocket and not in the world, who had tears in his own eyes for the long ride home and his son who pressed himself against the door at the far end of the long bench seat. It was a revelation to me, holding my Adam's little body in my arms, how my father felt it so intensely every time I withdrew myself from him, how abandoned he felt, how lost.

I saw the vulnerable five-year old that was me; I saw the stubborn adolescent; I saw the teenager raging out of the house with a scowl. In a moment of clarity I saw my own sons and how they would hurt me, drag me through the mud of love to some other country, some other person waiting to take my skin. I hugged my son so hard that he woke for a second, put his hand upon my cheek, and drifted back to sleep.

Poetry: 1980-2016

The Boy The Brave Girls

A pregnant woman in pink
Comes to the water
Behind her a tiny girl
In a yellow leather bikini
Follows, talking to her friends
And holding the hand of a
Timid boy, her brother
He loves being with the girls, tries
To be courageous around them
But the girls pull him into the sea
And when the water reaches
His waist he screams, struggling
To find the shore, wild-eyed,
Weeping
The girls are not upset by this
They surround him;
Saying "It's okay, it's okay."
And lift him up away from the sea.

The boy smiles, transformed
The brave girls
How wonderful they are, how true
He wants to be with them forever

In Bright Summer

In bright summer
we picked peaches
for hours, for days
each tree a dense house of hungry birds and bees
dipping sticky fingers into the sweetness of now
against the time when there would be none
Every farmer knows scarcity
Every farmer knows hope
This is the lesson my father taught me
Walking for hours behind his jenny mule
Standing in the doorway waiting for rain
Praying over his field and our food and sometimes
over me

On Cold Mornings, A Valentine To Ilana

We share a circular language
Our arms in arc to each other
The gravity, specific, of desire.

I wake to light with your
Breasts embracing my chest
Your thin feet penetrating my ankles
The rounded arch of my foot, my
Inner thighs

On cold mornings

You come to bed inside a chilled skin
We radiate together such an intense heat
I have to cast off the covers
When you undress my body smiles
Opens like a flower
my pollen enters
The room and pleases you
Gift enough for me to weep
To soften towards you in every extremity
But one

Brazil To Uruguay, 2012

Cast by the wind to Montevideo
I realize
That every city in the world
Has something for me
A park where the people and the green
Gather in some kind of ancient revolutionary agreement
A bar I want to inhabit each rich translucent day
A family I could love
And have love me
A shining flower I have never seen
An object that demands to be carried away
A music that moves me toward my hidden generous self
A tragedy so dark that I can never overcome it
No matter how large my heart
A heart so large it hears me whispering in a foreign tongue
And answers
A pair of eyes I cannot seem to discard
A poverty so deep it dismembers me
Opens me like a surgery
And shares divinity's regard for humanity
Where generosity
Is gathered like a ripe fruit in the meanest,
The meanest of circumstances
And ignored
By the people who rule this world so badly

3 Poems For Poetry On Buses

Accidental Poem: Answering the Emcees Questions

1.
Motivated by moonlight, the soft call of the mourning dove, poetry, courage and abiding love.

2.
I try to be an honest witness to my times, to live in a sacred manner, to love well and long, to be true and work my way to usefulness.

3.
I knew one afternoon in the hills of the Blue Ridge that nature is alive. I was five.

Visitation

Writing a poem at midnite, the air saturated with gardenia: flying squirrels raiding the feeder. Milky-white underbellies, airfoil tails, round dark saturated eyes. They are triangulating distances in mid-air. They are collecting mushroom spores to disperse into new territories. They are building a charnel house in the neighbor's attic. All this the young confess, eating pecans on the wide windowsill. Gliding away, they stretch their patagiums like sail work, fly.

Migration

Standing on her porch after a long frustrating day in hospitals: gibbous moon translucent in the east, sky open and full of color:
Hundreds of blackbirds cross my vision in rising darts, then a handful of arguing crows, and into the sun a vee of sleek dark ducks;
Such purpose! My mother is migrating too
Winged, hungry, hopeful; like a fledgling aiming the arrow of her body toward a home she's never seen.

The Visit

I come from a people
So deeply bedded in place
My grandmother wrestled her chair
Like one confined the whole hour or two
Or long afternoon but never the night
Love of grandbabies forced her
To come down the lea side of Mitchell
Off an unnamed tributary of Big Creek
In the Cane River watershed of
The upper Nolichucky of the big Atlantic
She had never seen, down
Just one simple road but over 3000 feet in elevation
To our house, not even in the flatlands then but
Piddling hills, red clay, wage slavery, paved roads:
She said: Ain't it hot?
Your water tastes a little funny.
Do you think we fed the mule before we left? Ain't it about
Time we went home, Bob?
After she said, spread-skirt: How's grandma's boys?
I love you I love you I love you

As an Old Man,
Grieving With Rachel In The Blacks

For Betty Lou Valentine

Me: first one up
Out the door
Pulling my boots on at the cold step

Above the laurel a galax cliff
Young sentinels of poplar
Witch-hazel making its own candescent winter light

In the next valley
A long train whistle:
Hearing it fills me with longing

Yesterday I made a prayer bundle
Of all my woes
And watched them burn

That train
It's just one valley away.

Found Along The Banks Of The Toe River Where My Mother Was Born

turk's-cap lily
squaw root /bear corn
cardinal flower
wild hazel-nut
St. John's wort
rattlesnake orchid
crane-fly orchid
poke: queen of July
Joe-pye: queen of the meadow
flower-of-a-day
wild clematis
monarda: bee balm, Oswego tea
dog hobble
orange jewel weed
wild carrot
chanterelles (!)
 hoary mountain mint
 tall Sweet Williams
 boneset
wooly mullein
climbing pea
yellow root
wild yam
flowering spurge
stone root
there -
a doe with two turkey hens
eating apples at days end.

Bear Schools Deer In The Woodland Of My Soul

I am a big man, where once I was a tall boy, lean like a deer.
Now I am a bear
Lumbering through my life dipping into local trash cans settled solid
Like a bear I am grounded to the earth like a bear
I am sometimes on my knees sometimes on the run protective of young
Inclined toward trees willing to be intoxicated fearsome when angry
I weigh 240 pounds
When I was 28 I weighed 185
I can see both of these people when I look into the mirror
But when I walk out into the world one is hiding
I like beer particularly good beer
With only the slightest excuse I will fill myself with beer
Like a guest or a celebration or thirst or for any other reason
I asked my wife when I started gaining weight
She said: "When you resigned yourself to me"
Yes at some point in my life I gave up a lighter-than-air part of
myself
It wanted to go places I couldn't go
I've said most of my goodbyes looked into the windows of regret
I like being a bear
I'm a better basketball player than I was at 18
I walk many miles a week live in the country have a rich collection of
friends
And a loving family good work to do
Still I'm startled sometimes shamed by my bigness in a mirror
My 13-year old's best friend calls me his favorite old fat man
Food and drink are a refuge for my anxiety
I worry about my long term health
Make elaborate plans to walk more eat less take 3 months on the Appala-
chian Trail
Whatever, but the fantasies dissipate like an October mist and I'm left
Standing, still me
Lumbering toward the next trash can humming
Looking for some honey

Puerto Rico: For Montek

These scratchings on the page, these marks, my intimate wander-
ings into territories of dissonance and consonance, are not different
from the animal tracks my cousins followed in early time:
Words arrive from the same animus and will filter like rain into
earth and wind and water.
What life is teaching me
Is that we are not separate
That even language is both sensate and sensible
That our deepest hearts
Are singing the world
       Like a winter wren crepuscular
       Like a pounding sea
Like toads in a wet springhouse begging for sex
Like the rise and curve and slow demise
Of the mountain
Like the cloud
Which gathers itself and leaves
Then leaves again

To Wear Red Shoes: After Olga Nolla

I love being a man
To be 58 years old
To live my life without armor
To trust women
And have them trust me
To write my poems
To cook with men
To make exquisite food
Out of the simplest ingredients
To talk about hunger
With my women friends
To sleep with my wife, languid, sated, cradled
To dress in my own style
And prepare my own clothes
To dress with happiness and style
To wear red shoes
To cut my hair short and sensual
To sleep in the daytime
And roam until dawn
To dream of the poems I want to write
To read books written by women
And to talk with women in the market
And to work with women
Caring for the world
To listen as the rain collides with my tin roof
To be enveloped in thunder
To run the waves and fall into the sea
To tell Eve, you did the right thing
You are doing the right thing.

Up On Naked Ground

(A bluegrass song I wrote with Jesse when he was 6 years old)

Up in the mountains where I live
There's a bald that's old and round
And from its top you can see the world
Folks call it Naked Ground, yes
Folks call it Naked Ground.

And many's the night by the silvery moon
That I played lost and found
Chasing friends and foes by the prickly rose
Up on Naked Ground
Up on Naked Ground.

When I gave my heart with a powerful start
-it was a love that knew no bounds.
We plied our tryst and made our list
Up on Naked Ground
Up on Naked Ground.

If we fill our lives with fear and hate
To our greed we will be bound
Til we open our hearts to the root of the world
And stand on naked ground, yes.

Til we stand on naked ground.

Living Alone

My grandmother Lilly
Grew up just light enough to pass
But not to matter; married at 13
Made her life a torch of love and raised 8 babies on nothing
But what they could scratch and raise and kill
Buried a husband in her 60s Come live
with us! Her children chimed, but she said no
Bought a used trailer first house she ever had with a bathroom
moved it around: Gastonia, Indian Trail, Green Creek
Little side yards of the people who had reason to love her
Aunt Lena's
husband died in a fiery crash
baby in her arms and one in the belly
She was a handsome
Sinewy whiskey-drinking woman of the hills
had other offers to marry but said
no. Do it twice?
kept an oiled rifle near to hand
Lived by a trout stream and took her water from a spring
Ate more wild meat than grocery goods - made
squirrel dumplings that drew the neighbors like
Pollinators to a hooraw bush
Taught school for 40 years with all her heart
Went home to meet her Jesus satisfied
Bending under the waters of the Primitive Baptist Church
Just in case.
Mrs. Cantrell lived down an off-lane near the end
of our dirt road
sweet cottage with a shaded porch under tall cool cedars
not our chaos but a place where everything had a place
my father took her to church and I used to visit her
bent gnarled kind shy
had a game laid out on the table when I came by
parched peanuts in the oven
She held both my hands whenever I left
As if to calm a stray animal and turn it loose
When she died I wept into the black telephone
A grown man a thousand miles away

Watching the pasture
that divides my two nearest neighbors
Widows living in houses they raised
a family and endured a husband in
Alive, wily, come into their own.
Maybe I can go sit with them today,
carry some sweet corn and shuck it
I'll say this
Sometimes a woman
has a seed of waiting
Imbedded in her by circumstance and blood
Her life a long
Exhalation of birthings until
the last one out of the canal is herself alone
Sufficient
Reveled in solitude
how I love and cherish them
Their beacon, their amplitude, their ripe sanctuary.

Creative Resistance

Letter From Deia: Why I Travel

After a last-minute flight cancellation and over 24 hours of continuous transport, changing planes in Toronto, Frankfurt and Barcelona, we arrived on Robert Graves' sun-kissed and rock tumbled island off the Spanish coast. At the summer house of my friend Andre, who produces plays in London and New York. We've known each other since our teens. I love him and his whole riotous family.

From this table I can watch the sea while I write, the slow play of light and clouds above the long horizon, the azure water as it sifts and moves and changes under the sky. A ring of mountains surrounds us, where the trees are carob and cedar and caper, with yucca and rosemary and even agave blooming out of cleft and crevice.

The household is just beginning to stir, but we early ones are quiet and respectful of each others' privacy, making tea and cutting fruit, starting coffee, turning to novels and journals and the hesitant tenuous beginnings of conversation, which within hours will become a strong communal stream and by evening a torrent of laughter, insights, feelings, advice, stories, suggestions and plans.

Yesterday was wet and cool, unheard of in August. We made a band of ten and walked over to the small town of Soller, 6 or 8 miles away, navigating a path between the Serra de Tramuntana and the Iberian blue. We saw several sweeps of the sea, terraced olive fields and citrus groves, walking sometimes through peoples' side gardens and sometimes over goat fences, everywhere companioned by a thousand years of stone walls, stone paths, stone houses, stone huts decorated with solar arrays and lime green reservoirs.

About two miles out of Soller we lunched at an 18th century estate by the side of the path, the C'a Xorc Hotel. Fare was tender ceviche, fresh salads and a rich brothy paella with tiny clams, hake-fish, octopus and pork, all taken with about 6 bottles of a good white wine. Fortified, Jamie and Millie and I left the others to cars and walked down the mountain to Soller, crossing the small-gage railroad track near where it tunnels under the mountain. We met the train at a bridge near the town, 7 wooden cars and a few passengers from Palma. The engineer waved and blew his whistle.

I felt happy, blessed by the sea, by good company, by the little town below us, by the friendly whistle of a lonely train on its way to the mountain.

Looking At My Country From 3000 Miles Away
Porto Alegre, Brazil 2014

(Sitting in the corner room by the street, the "nosy neighbor's room" Ilana says, with its leafy privacy and perfect view of the neighborhood, two expansive windows, a subtle overhang . . .)

I'm feeling the need to write a longer piece, add pictures to the remembering, the dis-membering of the voices of history and empire, the re-membering of being human and alive and in the foreign streets of Porto Alegre, Brazil in the early 21st century.

The poetry ringing in my ears demands it. The dispossessed demand it, filling every shadow, walking the streets in amplitude and sleeping under alcoves brave and visible.

We read the morning papers for news of home. They tell us that Americans have decided to export brown people without papers or powerful friends. They say the congress believes the war is just, the bomber a Muslim, the economy the point. In rising voices they plead with us to close our eyes and purchase amnesia, for the common good.

My love and I shout at the television, tell her family about my beloved queer family, write an email to a racist governor, agree from a great distance to plan an event, support a student, publish an essay, comfort a family . . . We do this with a certain heart but no certainty. Just pennies cast in a pool, petals on the wind, trying to be our best selves, to the biblical shout: Choose Life!

Moving now to a cafe, enjoying the unearned privilege of sitting still and watching humanity sort itself out in an urban hive: kindness and venality vie, the shadows lengthen, flowers of tropical trees demand attention, the coffee is good.

I have a copy of "A Wild Patience Has Taken Me This Far" burning a hole in my lap. Adrienne Rich's is a cornerstone, prickling my deepest love into usefulness, sometimes into a rich wild fury. She makes me verklempt, surprises my solitude like a choir of pagan cherubs. I am reading her aloud to taste the words and drive them home and make the world as it should be, whole:

with whom do you believe your lot is cast?
If there's a conscience in these hills
it hurls that question
unquenched, relentless to our ears
wild and witchlike
ringing every swamp

My Beautiful Aunt Zillah

My aunt Zillah died this week. She was my daddy's oldest sister.

This is a picture of her and my granny with the family cow, at age 13, taken in 1940. I like the way she fills out her overalls and how sullen she looks.

She was ever her own person and she loved me unconditionally, a comforting and always welcoming presence in my childhood.

Zillah was born into a share-cropping family and became a teenager between the the Great Depression and the Great War. The Phillips' were so poor they sent their children to school without shoes and Zillah worked like a man - sometimes plowing 14 hours a day behind a mule - until she was in her 30s. She and my dad were close in the way sometimes people are who have gone through very hard times together, and his eyes shone with a special light whenever she was around.

My aunt Zillah had a great horselaugh and a way of throwing her head back and raising her arms in hilarity or disgust. When she was serious she was serious and had intense heart-to-hearts with my momma which resolved always into tears or belly laughs, both of which seemed to come from the same rich abiding place.

One of the stars in the constellation of my life is missing, and I can feel a kind of loss of gravity, as I go about my life in a world that has so little to do with her or her experiences. Her final gift to me is the gift of tears, holding my momma, sitting in the little redneck Baptist church for the funeral and now pouring over my keyboard. I am sure the belly laughs will come too, sometime.

Chuck Tillotson

I dreamed of him as a bird last night,
migrating in the dark toward some vast coastal outline.
Other fliers joined as we flew.
Up ahead somewhere I could hear raucous welcome cries
and what sounded like a thousand gossiping voices.
Chuck made for it.
He shook me off somewhere
over the noisy shore with a tender but definitive dip,
and I woke up in my own body.
There were gold finches at the feeder, explosions of yellow energy
so intense that it took me long hollow seconds to recognize them as
being part of the real world.

((((((((((((((((((

Chuck Tillotson was a carpenter, a guitar player, a legendary party
boy. He laughed a lot, admired his friends and stayed true to them,
gave himself freely to strangers. He was a father to beautiful boys.
Chuck played a slow style of poker that drove some people crazy.
He was a handsome man with a gentle mien and a long unruly
white mustache. He had a voice like hot honey: low, whiskey-fil-
tered, languorous and warm.

Chuck had a great love in his life, his wife Veronica. They had
struggles, as all great loves do, but many people envied the laughter
they carried together and their love gravity, the way they leaned
toward each other over and again as if they shared a rich warm
secret.

(((((((((((((((((((

Chuck was alive and living his life and then he was in trouble and
then he was slipping away from us, one foot on the Long Road and
no more than a slim thread connecting him to the dirt and sweat
and precious air of this world.

Sharon Harris Nucl...

*In the unlikely event of an emergenc... sirens located in the 10 mile emergency planning zo... plant would be activated to alert the public.**

We came to Sharon Harris like tourists, dressed up, jolly – 3
Chatham County commissioners and our clerk, Sandra Lee, who was de-
lighted to leave her office and have an excursion with "the boys."

Actually, it was my second visit to Sharon Harris. The first had been
in the 1970's, when I was smuggled in by a friend who ran one of the 20-30
electrical crews desperately trying to finish the plant. It was one of the most
disorganized scenes I've ever witnessed, with several thousand workers
crawling over the construction site like ants, no visible order and the at-
mosphere of a giant party. At one time during construction Sharon Harris
employed more people than the entire population of Pittsboro.

*Plan ahead! It is a good idea to drive your evacuation route now so
that you are familiar with it.**

We arrived in the middle of the day, driving for 20 minutes with the
cooling tower in view, that nuclear icon made famous by Three Mile Island,
its billowing plume of white steam rising upwards like an animated brush
stroke, continuous, massive, indefatigable.

To enter Sharon Harris is to enter a compound, a fortress with
6-foot thick concrete walls, vast underground rooms, barbed-wire en-
closures, elaborate and redundant security procedures and a pyramidal
structure of command. A substantial private army roams the grounds
with federally permitted M-16s and full flack jackets, tense in their duties,
always on the alert.

*Watch a movie in Sparky's Amp Theatre to learn more about nuclear
fuel, plant operations or electrical safety.**

First we were greeted by two perky blonde women who identified
themselves as "community relations managers," then we were offered lunch:
fresh sandwiches and fat brown cookies. We were joined by a score or so
of CP&L employees, from shy engineers with pocket protectors to smiling
Vice-Presidents, mostly men, all Caucasians. Those of higher rank wore

The doctor called us in for a conference, into a lounge so full of people some had to share chairs or sit on the floor. He brought in his whole nursing crew for support. The doctor was gentle and his eyes misted, which comforted us, but his message was unequivocal. "I could do an intervention here," he said. "It's what we're trained to do as doctors. I could maybe give Chuck two or three more weeks, stem the infection with surgery and powerful drugs, but it would all come to the same thing, and I don't think Chuck would want us to do that." He blinked.

In a room just a few yards away Chuck lay, sedated and pierced with tubes. He looked so vulnerable it broke our hearts.

Veronica took her courage in hand and made the decision: Chuck would be taken off life support and his family would gather and make him as comfortable as possible. She talked with his sons and their strong fine mother, called family members, made arrangements with the nursing staff, had a final consult with the doctor.

I stood in for the family during the extubation, while the doctor and staff freed Chuck from his coil of tubes and separated him from the respirator. This procedure took over an hour. Nurses and doctors were tender and respectful, talking with Chuck as if he were conscious and making every effort not to cause him pain. They treated him always as a human being, as the treasure of a person we all knew.

At calm times during the procedure I worked with Chuck, and the staff gave me room. I blessed him with water and sang songs and prayers of release from many traditions, like this from The Pagan Book of Living and Dying:

Beloved Chuck, you are dying
But you are not alone.
We are here with you,
The beloved dead await you.
You go from love
into love.
Carry with you
only love.

Now my father speaks through my bones in the morning dew and sometimes Chuck Tillotson will slip into my dreams. I'm glad for both, and all that went before.

))))))))))))))))))))

survivors.
surrounded by dignity and love and community support for the ness somehow, not that they happened but that both deaths were were hard and shattering to me but they each had a sense of right-kindness to our family. Both these deaths, Chuck's and my father's, of its own, with food and witness and stories and a thousand acts of and I saw a conservative Baptist community I had fled taking care My sweet daddy died this year as well and almost as unexpected,

))))))))))))))))))))

ours, not yet.
us toward that Other Shore so close we could almost see it, but not broke out, with music, dancing and another raft of tears, floating ing on the Chatham/Alamance line and a riotous emotional wake That same evening Chuck's friends met at a community build-
aft   o have their time with Chuck and with the family.
    d-off, with 20-30 more waiting in the hall who came in
until he died. We all cried a bucket of tears but it was
    ugged him and whispered to him and held him
ae clean and comfortable his boys and Veron-

))))))))))))))))))))

Chuck,
od and said: "Chuck,
y man to inspire such love,

dark suits and interesting ties. I liked best the engineers and middle managers; they were proud of their work and their plant.

For this portion of the visit I sat with a NRC safety inspector, a steel-jawed man who bristled when I suggested that there was a public perception of his agency as a biased advocate for the nuclear industry. In fact, he took such umbrage at the remark that a community relations manager had to intervene and calm him down, saying: "Remember, the commissioner just said 'public perception.'"

(In Case of a Serious Emergency) 9. If you must go outside, place a cloth over your nose and mouth. *

After a flurry of handshakes we prepared for the tour, which involved almost an hour of security procedures. Dosimeters were hung around our necks to register radiation and we were told sternly to stay always with our guides. When Sandra was separated for a moment behind locked doors she was surrounded immediately by security guards.

Everything in the underground was clean as Disney World, which for some reason frightened me more than the security procedures. We were shown several restricted areas, including the now-famous fuel pools and the tense control room where a score of engineers in white shirts and ties anxiously watched and adjusted dials. There was something of the '60s about the whole atmosphere. The next day a technician accidentally shut the entire plant down, or so I gathered from a mysterious report in the N&O.

I remember standing near the fuel pools and watching my dosimeter click to "1," a small amount of radiation but a reminder of the invisible danger seeping from this fortress of power so close to my county, my home.

I was thoughtful during most of the tour, even more so on the drive back to Pittsboro. While I respect and admire the men and women who work at Sharon Harris I do not have the same confidence in CP&L's upper level management. Over the years they have proven to be self-protective, secretive and more interested in their profits than in the safety of the citizens of North Carolina.

79

For some reason the elaborate security procedures did not comfort me. For some reason I was not assured by the easy talk about fail-safe systems and nuclear transports surviving high-speed crashes intact.

My dosimeter clicked. I could feel my teeth ache as they do during dental x-ray. All the earnestness in the world could not make me feel safe there, near the fuel pools at Sharon Harris.

(* All quotations from Harris Plant Safety Information pamphlet)

Midnight Ramble

Leaf said it was a *life-saving rain* but not a *thriving rain*. It was true that it came too little and too late, and the salamanders did not move under our feet, but following the water from puddle to creek I tripped across three astonishing gifts: the luminous green shoots of wild garlic exulting, the fluttering winter wren startled from her cave in a muddy bank and one tiny cricket frog of all the vast chorus who let us see him, his pointed green nose and black eyes, see him fill his belly with his song
 and sing it.

Our Beautiful Argiope Is dying.

She has guarded her eggs with her last strength. Now she rests against the stabilimentum, a dense white zig-zag of silk she made to turn away birds and bats.

Corn Spider, Orb-Weaver, writing spider, mother of thousands: this picture shows her with her mate, so much smaller, who seduces her by plucking her web and then running to the safety of his own line nearby, over and over again until she softens to him. He makes a web at the corner of hers but dies soon after their affair.
Perhaps she ate him.

Her Great Work is done.

Under the cover of night she wove down a blanket of silk and then laid her eggs upon it, hundreds of them. She covered her babies with another layer of silk and then twirled the material with her legs into a perfect ovoid and hung it above her web, high in the corner of the doorway. Twice she did this.

They will not hatch until spring, her tiny ones.

On a warm day they will emerge out of the sac with purpose. Some few will remain near the homeplace but thousands will exude a strand of silk and ride the wind with it, no matter how far it takes them.

A Warm December In Silk Hope

We are drowning in rain this warm December and
every green thing lifts its head to first sun.
The feeder is occupied by woodpeckers and cardinals;
the flooded creek a chorus of cricket frogs.

Night before last we slept in the teahouse and
listened to the conversation of screech owls,
unbelievably tender and tremulous.

First light, I'm putting on muddy boots to follow the goddess,
wherever water flows.

...s The Wood Below Our House.

...all, the rough driveway is lined with huge red cedars, rem-
nants of a 100 year-old fence row. The largest are over 50' tall. Along
the edge of the house and pointing toward the creek is another fence
row, populated with dogwood and young water oaks and rich sas-
safras, all chaotically stretching toward any available light.

In a band above our little creek there runs a field of 20-30 year old
loblolly pines, the memory of an abandoned pasture still in evidence
along its margins: warm grassy patches bordered with berry vines,
stone piles, barbed wired nailed to a post oak.

The banks of the creek host maples and sweet gum and tag alder,
with a few paw paws for grace. A black willow stands in its own
patch of sunlight below the garden, bordered by wild persimmons
and one feral pecan tree. It's good to walk in the shade there, among
the tanagers and jays.

My favorite site is the small floodplain on the other side of the log
bridge, grounded by a huge maple and a grove of ancient water oaks.
The first time I walked there with my friend Leif Diamant we were
met by a pair of pileated woodpeckers swimming from tree to tree. I
thought: "I could live here."

This is no wilderness or pristine place. Everywhere there is evidence
of human activity, even mismanagement. But this little forest is
within my view from the kitchen table, always mysterious, surpris-
ing and changeable. It is precious to me. I try to love it as best I can.

My Favorite Forest Is The Wood Below Our House.

First of all, the rough driveway is lined with huge red cedars, remnants of a 100 year-old fence row. The largest are over 50' tall. Along the edge of the house and pointing toward the creek is another fence row, populated with dogwood and young water oaks and rich sassafras, all chaotically stretching toward any available light.

In a band above our little creek there runs a field of 20-30 year old loblolly pines, the memory of an abandoned pasture still in evidence along its margins: warm grassy patches bordered with berry vines, stone piles, barbed wired nailed to a post oak.

The banks of the creek host maples and sweet gum and tag alder, with a few paw paws for grace. A black willow stands in its own patch of sunlight below the garden, bordered by wild persimmons and one feral pecan tree. It's good to walk in the shade there, among the tanagers and jays.

My favorite site is the small floodplain on the other side of the log bridge, grounded by a huge maple and a grove of ancient water oaks. The first time I walked there with my friend Leif Diamant we were met by a pair of pileated woodpeckers swimming from tree to tree. I thought: "I could live here."

This is no wilderness or pristine place. Everywhere there is evidence of human activity, even mismanagement. But this little forest is within my view from the kitchen table, always mysterious, surprising and changeable. It is precious to me. I try to love it as best I can.

A Warm December In Silk Hope

We are drowning in rain this warm December and
every green thing lifts its head to first sun.
The feeder is occupied by woodpeckers and cardinals;
the flooded creek a chorus of cricket frogs.

Night before last we slept in the teahouse and
listened to the conversation of screech owls,
unbelievably tender and tremulous.

First light, I'm putting on muddy boots to follow the goddess,
wherever water flows.

Sassafras

Sassafras: outside my writing window in her incandescent colors. One of my favorite trees; fragrant, sympodial, medicinal, magical. 3 different leaf patterns: oval, lobed and mitten-shaped. Excellent firestarter because of its essential oil safrole, which is used in the making of MDMA. The source of gumbo file too.

Sassafras was one of the most significant American trade items in the 17th century, prized in the Old World as a cure for syphilis and gonorrhea.

A circle of Sassafras leaves wards off evil spirits. Phoebes, wild turkeys and pileated woodpeckers all consume their berries in medicinal quantities. Makes a great toothpick.
Abrade the twig bark and smell sarsaparilla.

I love Living In A Rammed Earth House.

It's dry, tight as a drum, lovely, and ignores severe weather changes. The materials didn't come from China, just soil from down the road and local pine, lovingly gilded by friends and Chatham County artists.

Real estate appraisers tell me that modern construction techniques will build a house that usually survives 20-40 years. We have a solid square of four hundred year earth walls under a beefy metal roof, sitting on a stem wall foundation that meets earthquake code. I can find structures built like ours all over the world: Han Dynasty watchtowers from 200 BCE, ancient farmhouses in southern France, a 19c church in lowcountry South Carolina, an experimental village in Alabama from the 1930s.
Still standing. Providing shelter.

It wasn't that expensive to build. Choosing small-scale construction and contracting the house myself meant that I could afford custom cabinets, hand-built tile counters, 10-foot ceilings, a stone courtyard. And the basic material is: cheap as dirt.

How can I say how warm it feels to be sheltered by 2 feet thick earth walls? Our house is welcoming and filled with light, decorated with carved sculpture niches and long ambling striations of color, cluttered by the regular stuff of our lives but anchored like a rock to the earth, to a commonality so rich it sings to me every day.

It's as basic as basic can be.

James Still And Lena Holloway Fagan

I have been thinking a lot about death and loss and transition. My father died this year and I lost some good friends and I am often in mourning over the destruction we lay upon the long-suffering earth, it's precious hills and valleys.

James Still of Kentucky. He was 94 years young and still writing. One of his most recent poems was entitled "Those I Want in Heaven With Me Should There Be Such A Place."

James Still was a mountain of a literary figure who decided not to write about the world at large but to write about the world at hand: his farm, his land and his neighbors. He was the Poet Laureate of Kentucky.

In the early 1930's Still took the first money he ever made from a short story (It was $500 from the Saturday evening Post and his father said: "They must have meant $50.") and settled into an ancient log house off Little Carr creek in Knott County, Kentucky. To get there you had to ride or walk eight miles of dirt track road and walk up two miles of creek bed.

James Still was college educated and well traveled but he was plain as dirt. James made himself right at home in Knott County, working his patch of garden there for over 60 years. One of his neighbors was said to say: "You talk smart but you got hillbilly wrote all over you."

I first heard of James Still from my Aunt Lena, a schoolteacher in Yancey County, North Carolina. Aunt Lena was a fierce and unrepentant mountain woman who hunted deer and fished for trout in the creek outside her house, and I loved her. She had this poem taped to her bathroom wall:

Heritage

I shall not leave these prisoning hills
Though they topple their barren heads to level earth
And the forests slide uprooted out of the sky.

Though the waters of Troublesome, of Trace Fork,
Of Sand Lick rise in a single body to glean the valleys,
To drown lush pennyroyal, to unravel rail fences;
Though the sun-ball breaks the ridges into dust
And burns its strength into blistered rock
I cannot leave. I cannot go away.

Being of these hills, being one with the fox
Stealing into the shadows, one with the new-born foal,
The lumbering ox drawing green beech logs to mill,
One with the destined feet of man climbing and descending,
And one with death rising to bloom again, I cannot go.
Being of these hills I cannot pass beyond.

James Still was a mountain man from his heart to his big feet. He loved to tell a joke about a group of Appalachian people who had to be fenced in an off-section of Heaven; they tried to go home on weekends. He did not consider death to be a foe or something to be feared. He was well past 90 when he was asked about his notion of dying by a neighbor at the local store. With a grin, James Still quoted Ben Franklin: "Death is as natural as sleep. We will arise refreshed in the morning."

The Conference On Money and Meaning

I was speaking in my head to Dorothy Parker and she said:
"If you wanna know what God thinks about money just look at the
people he gives it to."

In Guanajuato they like to say: *Dios les da el dinero a los ricos.*
It's a good thing God gives money to the wealthy "because without
it they would starve to death."

So I'm saying there's a lot of Money without Meaning out there
But how do we make a path toward meaning; how do we as people
and entrepreneurs and citizens and lovers hold ourselves account-
able to our responsibilities and our vision, to our need and our love,
to our families of belonging and the Earth to which we belong?
How do we engage with joy?

Some people say money is just a vehicle I say it is a 1957 Chevy
with bad shocks and no brakes; looks good on the outside but that
sucker can kill you.

My father grew up in the last non-cash economy of America, in a
sharecropping subsistence that translated to 14 hours a day walking
behind a mule's ass. He left that world to work half a century in cot-
ton mills. When I asked him why he put aside 10% of every meager
paycheck for the Southern Baptist church he said: "That money's
not mine; it belongs to the Lord."

We lived in a four-room house without benefit of indoor bathroom
but we were not poor.

Wendell Berry writes that "To have everything but money is to have
much."

Here, in this room and in this community, we have pleasures that
money can't buy and corporations can't command.

We have each other; we have a local economy of shared work; we
have comfort when we need it. We have our stories, our long his-
tory in this bioregion. We are producers instead of consumers of

meaning. This is important.

I have many disagreements with our industrial economy. It tends to value private profit over public good, speed and efficiency over enjoyment and quality, utility over mystery and meaning. Ah! Meaning, again.

I hate that it does not account for affection, therefore it does not account for value, that it tends to destroy what it cannot understand, that it is based on the invasion and pillage of the earth and the poor.

I hate it that the same 400 families that sent out armadas 400 years ago to colonize the world still control most of the world's wealth.
There are practical and elegant and redemptive alternatives:
The business I founded is celebrating 33 years. We feed 10 families, allow part-time work at full-time scale, function as a team, have transparent books, own our own building, have never been capitalized, share profits with the community, try to be on the right side of history, have a primary environmental ethic in a field that is not famous for one . . .

I understand that every human enterprise requires factual knowledge, calculation and manipulation - we like to say we "run the numbers,"

But a real and lasting economy as well as a good business proceeds by
Humility,
Sympathy
Forbearance
Generosity
And Imagination.

Let us remember and remind the corporatocracy that the root word of property is proper, which includes right relationship. And Economy? Economy was diminished to mean money and its accumulation of power.

The true meaning of economy is "the arrangement of households."
So let us arrange our households together in a way that provides for the general not specific prosperity, that honors the Earth and the path of social justice, that brings us into right relation with others and the world, that provides in every workspace a living place of creativity, shared purpose, well-being and by that course deep and abundant wells of meaning.

The Difficulty And The Gift I Carry Toward Death
(Also known as Apology to Leif and Ilana)

(I come to this writing task like a man who faces a machinery he might lose a finger to, like a kosher butcher who makes her prayers to God with fear and trembling, afraid they might be answered.)

Last night I went to bed bruised and blue, as I have for several days. I perceive now that I spoke sharply to my lover in a way that made her ambivalent about coming to bed with me, much less being tender with me, something I wanted so deeply I was afraid to ask for it.

I knew that my testiness and agitation, my ragged lack of patience, was connected somehow with an angry tumultuous conversation I had with my best friend yesterday, but I could not untangle my feelings from my reactions. They each withdrew from me a bit, friend and wife, wounded by my raging animus.

So I went to bed alone. At the door of sleep I floated inchoate questions:

What is my path forward or backward?
Where are the markers?
What restless spirit animates and endangers me?

The image which built itself piece by piece from that moment until it woke me at 3AM was whole and stark and piercing: my friend Ruffin's body broken on the rocks under his tall house and not found for hours, pelted at by rain and wind.

My dream body caught its breath and understood. Waking, I released the tears which had threatened to drown me whole.

So, here it is. I am a vulnerable man in my fifties, surrounded and permeated by loss (personal- ecological-political), not so much afraid of my own death as I am of my frailty, of the inevitable demise of the people I love, and of who I will be without them.

In this case, I wanted my beloveds to be present so deeply as a hedge against brother death that I tested them (my "testiness") with a sharper regard to see if they bled, to assure myself that they were not phantoms, that I would find them warm and connected to me in the sympathetic restless light of morning .

This is not unfamiliar to me. I know I can react this way to precipitous events, where I literally feel myself out over a chasm of change, of possibility, of a deep and necessary regret. This has been a year of so many funerals.

I want to solidify in the deepest possible way what is real in my life, but I don't have the right to fearfully rattle the cages of my relationships and frighten the people I love. I step back consciously from that precipice, set about repairing the bridge, commit to a generous daily life of support and engagement.

To the most important people in my life: This does not take you off the hook of my hard love. I have apologies to extract as well as give, conflicts to resolve in the context of relationship-building. I don't always like the way you do things or how you treat me, and I want us to talk with candor about our feelings. I promise to listen, and to be tender.

One of the legacies of death's corona is an urgency to talk about difficult issues, an impatience with the surface of things, a courage to dive into dark waters. I'm choosing to accept that gift. Life is short. Engage with me.

Creative Resistance

We will have to build that resistance from whatever comes to hand:
whispers and prayers, history and dreams, from our bravest words . . .
Derrick Jensen

I was born into a great sprawling multi-racial family that ran from
the mountains of North Carolina down to the Cherokee foothills
of South Carolina. We identified ourselves mostly as poor, South-
ern and white, but I knew from the time I was 5 or 6 years old that
the color line was more like my momma's clothes line, with a wide
range of shade flapping in that breeze. We were hill-and-mountain
people who lived in the open, hunters, farmers, preservers of food
and old stories. The legacy for me was a world where nature was
never outside somewhere but connected with strong cords to my
heart and my breath and to the soles of my feet, to the common
daily adventures of a wondrous world.

At major family gatherings I usually had a choice; I could go out
hunting and tinkering with the men or I could stay with the women
and the cooking and their stories. Often I held with the women,
and that shaped my life.

I am in a camp somewhere between Wendell Berry and Naomi
Klein, home-centered and nourishing but near to a rage at the stu-
pidity and culpability of the world being built around us: its extrac-
tive economy, sad patriarchy and grinding march toward empire.

These days I think of myself as a kind of spiritual janitor. I write;
I live in an elegant dirt-house built by people I love; I walk the
woods. I facilitate the transitions of organizations, negotiate the
transfer of land, carry water for strong women, create rituals and
perform liturgies. I bind people together and honor their dead. I
pray for the soil under my feet and call in the directions in ceremo-
ny; I listen to trees and every living thing. Sometimes I give a public
witness; sometimes it scares people. I give good solid advice. I love
my partner.

I cook, and I clean up.

Mary June Holloway

My sweet mother still lives in the house I grew up in, the last survivor of 10 rough-scrabble brothers and sisters. Hers was a high-mountain clan colored with Cherokee. They owned 46 acres of steep land above Big Creek in Yancey County and scratched out four of them to grow burley tobacco on. This paid the land taxes and bought the children shoes every winter. We have a family cemetery there that overlooks the creek valley and the old homeplace.

Grandpa Holloway was the last schoolteacher in Lost Cove, which was abandoned in the 1930s and the land turned over to Pisgah National Forest. Everybody walked out of that community together because it was too hard to make a living. At my grandpa's house I slept under a stack of quilts in a little room off the porch. Sometimes on full-moon nights he would wake me and we would let loose the coon hounds and follow them all night long. He taught me to be friends with the dark and in his presence I heard the wild call of wilderness.

Gurley Phillips

My father, a decent and loving man out of Pea Ridge, North Carolina, a care-taker of many, a storyteller. He grew up between the Great Depression and the Great War, the youngest son in a share-cropping family that was dirt poor. His father made him quit school in the 5th grade to walk 14 hours a day behind a mule. In his early 20's he took a job in a cotton mill, where he worked as a loom fixer for over 50 years. He kept a garden with a horse until his 60s and went to church every time the doors were opened. He liked to laugh and he wept when he prayed in public, which he was often asked to do.

Crossing The Color Line

My arc toward social and racial justice has often meant encounters with public violence and rejection. In my strongest hour I always seem to raise the devil against me. is has happened to me as a youth, as a pastor and as a politician

I gave my heart to the civil rights movement in 1971, sitting in a circle of rocking chairs at the Highlander Center in Tennessee. We all told our deepest stories, one by one. It quickened a charge in me.

Trained in non-violence, I hitch-hiked to demonstrations in Spartanburg, Greensboro and D.C., spoke up in churches and wrote strong editorials for anybody who would publish them. I found my-self in a boatload of trouble: the county sheriff came to our house to warn my daddy and the high school principal refused to process my scholarship application and a truckload of rough-looking men drove me all over Polk County one night to educate me about my responsibilities as a white citizen of the republic. I barely made it to graduation alive in 1972 and I have never considered moving back to Green Creek.

Becoming A Preacher

In the mid-1990s I was appointed the pastor of Mount Zion United Methodist Church in Pittsboro, which was one of the richest experiences of my life. It was a small congregation of mostly elders. We put a sign out at the end of the road that said "Come as You Are". I washed their feet, baptized their babies and buried their dead.

I developed a covenantal relationship with Elder Carrie Bolton of the United Holy Church, one of the great preachers of the South. She and I broke the color barrier in Methodist Churches throughout the region by holding joint services, using her extraordinary choir as a drawing card. At the same time I became involved in the movement for gay and lesbian inclusion in the church, meeting with other activists, pressing the message from the pulpit and offering to perform same-sex unions. These activities angered my local Board of Ordained Ministry, but it wasn't until I ran for county commissioner that they felt threatened enough to act. I was issued an ultimatum: abandon your public aspirations and tone down your activism or leave the pulpit. They withdrew my appointments and revoked my scholarship to Duke Divinity School, severing me from their fellowship and support. Kicked out of the church!

From this vantage, 20 years later, I can see it as an act of grace. I loved being a pastor but I was never exclusively a Christian; I hear an old horn at daybreak and the earth religions call to me with an insistence I would have had to reconcile at great cost. At the time, however, I wept myself to sleep and was lost for a whole season.

Not Acting Like A White Man

In 1998 I was elected as Chatham County's first environmental-ist Commissioner. It was a hard campaign; I unseated a 26-year incumbent to face an agri-business Republican who vowed hog lagoons were so efficient that you could drink the water from their outflow. At my victory celebration commissioner Betty Wilson, a treasure, offered me this prophetic statement: "Gary, I envy you so much! You don't have any enemies yet."

I led the charge to craft a strong land-use plan, which frightened the NC Homebuilders Association. We challenged developers in open session and started a dynamic public hearing process that often filled the courthouse. We created a human relations commission and made a bridge to the emerging Latino community, supporting dual-language programs, work equity, fair housing and access to services. We voted down an asphalt plant supported by our Congressman and refused to permit a massive subdivision on our northern border, standing together in unison to show our resolve.

My last year of office I could barely walk through town without being assaulted by supporters and detractors. The development lobby joined with the county conservatives and raised hundreds of thousands of dollars against my re-election, a sum that shocked local media. A Republican businessman switched his party affiliation to Democrat and bought a rough cottage in my district to oppose me. Republicans were encouraged to change their affiliation in order to vote against me in the primary. Some did.

My opponents selected a strategy of "chipping away at the dam," a myriad of actions designed to harm my reputation. There was a group who came to every commissioner meeting in 2002 and asked me publicly if I was a member of the Communist Party. I was in a time warp. "Gary Phillip's Seat under Siege from Well-heeled Outsiders" proclaimed the Chapel Hill Herald.

Meanwhile, I felt my center slipping from so much conflict. This is from my 2002 journal:

What about art, and the liquid sea of my life, and my religious call?

99

I feel flung around by unfriendly forces. I'm spending too much time in the shallow end: information, negotiation, facilitation, paperwork, and such shit. Maybe I need to rip away the skin of my public life, move away from this dry time, this dry work, this bucket of conflict . . .

One of the lowest points came when a group from the local Ruritan Club asked me to meet with them, farmers and mechanics and millworkers. I looked around the room and saw my uncles, my family, the rough fine people I had grown up with. "Gary, we can't vote for you this time," they said. "You just don't know how to act like a white man."

Well, I couldn't argue with that.

I lost the election by 320 votes. The Independent Weekly ran a special: "Sold Out: How Developers Bought Chatham County." Thousands upon thousands of housing lots were approved in short order, most of which became zombie subdivisions during the recession and housing crash.

My Grandmothers

I could never tell my story without introducing my grandmothers Lily and Etta, who I carry in ceremony and who each became the backbone and gristle of my life, imparting in a thousand ways the wonder of the world and my place in it. They are one of the reasons I feel at ease in working groups of women and know how to be a true friend.

Lily Price came out of South Carolina from a family that included many African-Americans. She raised 8 boys and girls on nothing more than what grew out of the ground in front of whatever farmhouse they lived in while they were growing crops for somebody else.

After her older boys disappeared into the army and her husband committed suicide she settled into a little trim mobile home and lived an independent life. Luckily this was not so far from us, and she and I were loving companions from the time I was in diapers. We talked about everything and she was my first true friend.

Grandma Etta Holloway could never abide being anywhere but in her high mountains, and any time she consented to visit us she was fidgety and ready to go home in an hour or two. I spent a large part of every summer following her around. Etta was a forager and herbalist who had a theory of wild "tonics" and cooked on a wood stove. She was a kind of kitchen witch, which I am. She was a magical creature who was brown as a berry, with hair that reached below her waist and a quick sure quiet way about her. I have seen her kill a chicken and pluck it clean before the water boiled to cook it in. She is my reminder ghost, sitting on my shoulder with a wry sense of humor as I go about in ceremony.

Writing And Ceremony In Service To The Wild

It's 6AM and I have come downstairs quietly to write. Later Ilana will call me back to bed and I'll slip under the covers with a quick joy, but now I have to concentrate on Winter Solstice, when I am organizing two services, one at the new Buddhist temple and one around the bonfire at Stone Circles, my favorite social justice retreat center. We will gather to birth the sun, to affirm the lessons of the dark and welcome the light, as peoples have done for thousands of years. One of my jobs is to prepare the wisdom teaching for Solstice.

This morning I'm inspired by the litany of all that is happening in the natural world on December 21, 2011, under our feet and above our heads and in every dark rich corner. I'm writing:

"Red-winged hawks are making a harvest of first-year squirrels now that the leaf cover is down and wood chucks and eastern chipmunks have dug to their winter sleeping lairs. Noisy flocks of crows and blue-jays and robins gather at the margin of fields. Red-backed salamanders are on the move and on sudden warm days American bird grasshoppers will rise and fly. The winter forms of the Hop Merchant butterfly have drunk their last drop of the year's sun and rest in diapause. Tiny screech owls are calling from the woods on still nights and soon yearling bucks will lose their antlers."

I have not yet written about the movement of the stars (Venus in Aquarius, the night sky dominated by marching Orion) or the winter green on the forest floor (crane fly orchid, rattlesnake plantain, wild ginger, pipsissewa . . .) or even the teeming lives under the leaf litter, but I will.

It is one of my disciplines, to try to use thick description to mark the turings of the natural world. The words I midwife spread like winter birds (brown creepers, hermit thrushes ruby-crowned kinglets, yellow-rumped warblers . . .) and have a life of their own.

Men's Work

In the winter of 1978 I moved with a group of friends to western Massachusetts to start an intentional community. We bought a farmhouse together in Pelham and the commune prospered for years, but the most enduring legacy of that time was a men's group I helped form which has met continuously for over 30 years.

This glittering band of men meets for a full day each month, plus a five day retreat in the fall on the St. Lawrence River. I meet with them whenever possible, collaborate with them continuously, and correspond with one or more of them almost every day. We called ourselves many things, from Men Against Patriarchy in the 80's to Men on Mushrooms in the 90's. Over the years we have published a film about our group, provided childcare for women's events, organized performance art against nuclear power, participated in civil disobedience, joined together to help build an experimental solar house and told each other our deepest personal histories over long slow weekends. We are still a rich part of each other's lives, of each other's lifework and personal struggles. Now we are growing older and dealing with health and end of life issues: we will stay engaged until the day we help carry each other to our burying grounds.

In this life-long process of struggle and pleasure we have become intimate with each other as men in a way that betrays the system of power and oppression and privilege more effectively than any one act or campaign or passionate ideal.

In a world dominated by patriarchy and its impulse for control, the fates of women and of people of color and of the earth are vulnerable to the same forces.

My life's work is devoted to the enterprise of connecting an inclusive community into a web of spiritual power strong enough to stand against empire. And one of the platforms of my life continues to be this group of men: Paul Richmond, poet and performance artist; Llan Starkweather, designer/futurist; Alan Surprenant, apple farmer and anti-nuclear activist; Tom Weiner, teacher and author; Stephen Bannasch, techno-nerd genius and instrument-maker; Dick McLeester, founder of Vision Works; Robbie Lepser, award-winning documentary film-maker; Stephen Trudel, counselor/men's healer and Tony Clarke, one of the world's great cabinetmakers.

The Community Of Women

I am now, in 2012, a member of 6 diverse women's groups.
None of these groups started out explicitly as women's groups; three
are public boards. It's just that often I find myself in a happy seri-
ous working coven of strong women, going about the restorative
work of the commons, doing what needs to be done. Having called
myself a womanist for over 30 years, I am now growing into the
deepest incarnation of that self-description.

In my book group we read novels and non-fiction organized
around issues of social and racial justice. The conversation is an
island of possibility where we take the chance to express ourselves
passionately. These are strong women, graduates of a state-wide
leadership program, each captains of their own industry. My wife
invited me to this group. It's juicy.

I'm part of a ritual group, a "worship committee" which gathers to
plan large events marking the wheel of the year, particularly the
equinoxes and solstices. We call our work "Gathering the Tribes"
and our clear intention is to create a wild and safe communal open
space where the seasonal, the celestial, the creative and the personal
can meet and pollinate each other. On a regular basis we break
bread and drink wine together, check in with each other and spend
hours "chopping wood and carrying water" in the work of our spiri-
tual commons.

I have a plant ally group that meets monthly. We have a wide net
and sometimes men actually attend this one. We are creating a
seasonal calendar for the gathering of wild edibles and medicines;
we share wild foods and explore the deeper narratives of plants.
We eat, we talk, we work, we walk somewhere nearby and explore
what's growing in our back yards and open spaces.

All these groups are church for me: intimate, positive, mysterious
and kind.

My public boards are Family Violence and Rape Crisis Services of
Chatham County, the Abundance Foundation and the Dogwood
Alliance. Of these only Dogwood has a significant percentage of

men on their board. John, Neville, Rod and Dan prove the exception to my experience that mostly it is women who show up.

Michael Meade published an article this year in Speaking Truth to Power titled "Where Have All the Wise Men Gone?" "We live in a time of great forgetting", he says, where precious life-sustaining elders are being replaced with just 'olders who fail to recommit to the great ideals that sustain the deepest values of human life . . .'

I find this so true of men in general, and it is a great source of sorrow for me. On the other hand, my life is rich with women who show up over and over again with a grounded vision, the courage of conviction and a willingness to self-sacrifice, luminous qualities of the elder.

I take a charge from the poet Adrienne Rich:

My heart is moved by all I cannot save
So much has been destroyed
I have to cast my lot with those
Who, age after age, perversely,
With no extraordinary power,
Reconstitute the world.

Grounding: Taking Root

Joanna Macy talks about a vital arc of ceremony: We begin in gratitude (because everything must begin in gratitude), actively honor our pain for the world, open up to new ways of seeing and then commission ourselves ('sally forth,' she says) to meet our destiny with an open heart.

My tale follows that arc. My wish is to grow up and then grow down, like a white oak or pignut hickory or southern chestnut. In half a century my personal totem has moved from deer to bear to turtle to tree. I hope to arrive at my sustainable best: standing firm, sheltering many and making mast.

May all the deities bless us in our comings and our goings. May we become indigenous together. Amen.

Acknowledgements

Quite a few of the occasional pieces here and several of the poems first appeared in Chatham County Line. (Avanti Media Consultants, LLC.) Thank you, Julian.

A previous version of the essays included in the last section of "Creative Resistance" was published as a chapter in Small Stories, Big Changes (2013, New Society Press), edited by my friend Lyle Estill and attended by a wonderful book tour.

"Leaving Earth" was workshopped with the generous and extraordinary support of Luis Alberto Urrea at the 2015 Orion/Breadloaf Writers Conference.

"Bear Schools Deer in the Woodland of my Soul" was first published by The Sun magazine.

"Chuck Tillotson" has been widely published and still produces several heart-felt letters a year by people who loved him.

"The Community of Women" and "The Way Love Circles" have both appeared under different titles on The Good Men Project.

I bow to my people of Appalachia, to the loving family that raised me, to my luminous sons, my many teachers, the living earth. And to my wife Ilana: collaborator, lover, found family.

I am deeply grateful to Pat Jobe, Tami Schwerin, Tom Weiner, Liora Mondlak and Ilana Dubester, who read the manuscript and offered suggestions. Most of all to my publisher Paul Richmond, one of my favorite poets, best friends and a constant source of inspiration.

Many others I hope I have thanked within these pages, by giving them the rich attention they deserve.

Gary Phillips

is the 2016-2018 poet laureate of Carrboro, North Carolina.

He is a writer, naturalist and entrepreneur.

Gary has a special interest and expertise in conservation easements and other land-protective strategies.

He lives in a rammed earth house with his wife Ilana Dubester in Silk Hope, North Carolina.

Gary avidly reads poetry and anthropological science fiction, studies amphibian activities on full moon nights and was once chair of the Chatham County Board of Commissioners.

He likes bourbon and is a child of Appalachia, a womanist, a singer.

Celisa Steele comments,

"It has been an honor to serve as Carrboro's poet laureate for the past three years," said Steele. "W.S. Merwin, who twice served as U.S. poet laureate, said, 'I think there's a kind of desperate hope built into poetry now that one really wants, hopelessly, to save the world. One is trying to say everything that can be said for the things that one loves while there's still time.' Gary is one of the most hopeful and loving poets I know," continued Steele. "He's ideal for the poet laureate role—for helping us to see the hope in the apparently hopeless. Carrboro is lucky to have him."

"Your words always feel like a balm to me."

Meredith Leight

"Such a writer. Such a storyteller. What a heart. What a soul."

Pat Jobe

"Poetry is not optional," Audre Lorde said to Gary Phillips in 1979, and he took it to heart.

Dani Moore

"I continue to admire and be so moved by your work."

Caren Stuart

"Blessings on Gary Phillips, on his exquisite depth of understanding, and to all who read this. I promise your day will be far more beautiful."

Beth Owls Daughter

"Absolutely beautiful. Your words and your understanding will not soon fade from my conscious and never from my heart. Thank you."

Mary Munger

"Absolutely beautiful...i can picture these strong, independent women in my mind's eye..."   Jerri M Henline